SAVING OAKY WOODS

John T Trussell

*To Jimmy —
Hope to see you in
Oaky Woods!
Best Wishes —
John T Trussell*

Copyright © 2018 John T Trussell

All rights reserved.

ISBN:1724547216
ISBN-13:9781724547217

DEDICATION

Saving Oaky Woods is dedicated to my wife Billie, sons Brandon and Trent and Grandkids Analyssa, Ava, and Jack. I also want to thank every person who hunted or trekked with me into Oaky Woods looking for natural beauty in the outdoors, talked with me in regard to news and tv stories or supported our efforts to Save Oaky Woods. We could not have succeeded without your support! Front cover photo courtesy of US Fish and Wildlife Service

Foreword by Pierre Howard, Past President, Georgia Nature Conservancy and former Lt Governor of Georgia.

"John Trussell was the most important and most consistent voice for preserving Oaky Woods. He lived and breathed it for a long time, and he deserves great credit for saving its most biodiverse reaches"

Pierre Howard

John Trussell, left, with Former Oaky Woods Manager Raye Jones, Wildlife Biologist Bobby Bond, and current Oaky Woods Manager Tommy Shover. These men, along with Kevin Kramer, Region Biologist Supervisor and former Supervisors Ken Grahl and Dick Whittington, deserve much credit for their fine work at Oaky Woods. Let's also appreciate the work of the former Oaky Woods Managers like Larry Ross and DNR Law Enforcement Officers who worked long hours for the public good

CONTENTS

	ACKNOWLEDGMENTS	i
1	OAKY WOODS IN THE BEGINNING	10
2	THE STATE SHOULD BUY OAKY WOODS	23
3	RUNNING WATER COMES TO OAKY WOODS	36
4	BLACK BEARS IN OAKY WOODS	40
5	MIDDLE GEORGIA BEARS- HOW MANY?	45
6	TWO BEARS TAKEN IN MIDDLE GA HUNT	63
7	CLYDE YODER'S TIPS FOR OAKY WOODS BUCKS	66
8	HUNT FROM THE GROUND IN OAKY WOODS	71
9	BIG BUCKS COME INTO OAKY WOODS AND OCMULGEE CHECK STATION	75
10	CLEAR CUT- WHERE'S THE DEER?	80
11	WILD RUSSIAN BOARS OF OAKY WOODS	85
12	PEACH STATES BEST BETS FOR WILD HOGS	92
13	DEALING WITH MARAUDERS IN OUR MIST	98
14	WINTER IS A GREAT TIME FOR SMALL GAME HUNTING	102
15	COUGARS IN OAKY WOODS AND GEORGIA?	107
16	OAKY WOODS, ONCE AT BOTTOM OF OCEAN, HAS RICH GEOLOGICAL HISTORY	114
17	THE DAY THE HEAVENS RAINED FIRE ON CENTRAL GEORGIA	119
18	THE CAVES OF CENTRAL GEORGIA	123
19	THE SAND DUNES OF CENTRAL GEORGIA	129

20	FISHING IN OAKY WOODS	131
21	A CHAMPION TREE GROWS IN BONAIRE	140
22	DO YOU HAVE A CHAMPION TREE ON YOUR LAND?	142
23	OAKY WOODS FIRE TOWER FADES INTO HISTORY	146
24	GOPHER TORTOISES ROAM OAKY WOODS	149
25	STATE PURCHASES A MAJOR PORTION OF OAKY WOODS	152
26	STORY BEHIND AMAZING 1862 BEECH CARVING	157
27	RARE PLANTS AND CHALK PRAIRIES OF OAKY WOODS	160
28	A HIKE IN OAKY WOODS	164
29	BE AWARE OF BEAR DANGERS	173
30	KNOWLES LANDING A GREAT ASSET TO MIDDLE GEORGIA	179
31	GEORGIA'S YAZOO LAND FRAUD	184
32	EXOTIC/ INVASIVE PLANTS IN OAKY WOODS	188
33	FLYING SQUIRRELS, SPANISH MOSS, CICADAS, MISTLETOE, HONEY SUCKLE, DOGWOODS AND SANDHILL CRANES	193

ACKNOWLEDGMENTS

This book is being written to provide a permanent record for a large tract of land that became known as OAKY WOODS Wildlife Management Area. In the past, Oaky Woods was owned by several major land owners and then leased to the state for outdoor recreation. Although Oaky Woods was established in 1966 for Georgia's hunters and anyone who appreciates nature, it became a political football in 1993 when Jay Walker, then a State Representative, proposed, along with several other politicians, that the state buy the property. Unfortunately, that effort fizzled out due to a lack of commitment from the State of Georgia.

Things heated up again in 2004, when the Weyerhaeuser Company, who owned the land at the time and leased it to the state, decided to sell all their Georgia timberlands, which was 322,615 acres. Undoubtedly, it was the largest transfer of private property in Georgia's recent history. In Crawford County, 37,511 acres went up for sale, the total in Houston County was 33,817 acres, which included much of Oaky Woods. The Georgia Department of Natural Resources had Oaky Woods listed as their top priority for purchase as a "legacy Tract". But when the Nature Conservancy of Georgia, led by Chairman of the Board Pierre Howard, a former Lt Governor of Georgia, offered to loan the state the necessary funds, with no time table to pay back the money, Governor Sonny Perdue and DNR Commissioner Lonice Barrett, refused the offer, saying that the state could not afford the deal. However, it was proposed that much of the purchase monies would be raised from donations and grants, with little or no cost to the state. With the state refusing an attempt to broker a deal with the Nature Conservancy and the Weyerhaeuser Company, the land went into the bidding process. Of course, the behind the scenes negotiations that when on at the time will never be known.

Private business interests, who bought the land, wanted to develop the land into up to 30,000 residential lots, while conservation interests wanted to preserve the land. It was the third largest and wildest property in Georgia, and once it was developed, its small and fragile black bear population, its rare plants and animals and its unique chalk prairies would be lost forever. This is the story of the battle for Oaky Woods, plus a lot of information about its rich natural resources.

Pierre Howard, center, President of the Georgia Nature Conservancy and former Lt Governor of Georgia, toured Oaky Woods with John Trussell, right, and Will Wingate, Legislative Director, left, and gave very valuable assistance in the effort to preserve Oaky Woods.

When I started "Save Oaky Woods", I asked some select private individuals to partner with me to mount a positive public relations campaign to convince the state to buy Oaky Woods as a part of its Wildlife Management Area Program. But we had a problem in that we had no money! It's hard to finance anything selling t-shirts, bumper stickers and yard signs; we were truly a grass roots effort!

Some people turned me down, saying I had about a zero chance of success and it would snow in middle Georgia in July before the state bought Oaky Woods from the private developers. I knew that they might be correct!

However, I knew that a few years before, I had been successful in working with the Houston County Commissioners in renovating the Houston County Boat Ramp at highway 96. After many years of neglect, I was able to spearhead the effort because it was something that was seriously needed in the community and I thought the County Commissioners would be supportive. They did support the effort and we re- built the 96 boat ramp. As an outdoorsman, Outdoor Writer and experienced governmental employee, I thought that I could work with others to get the job done. Saving Oaky Woods seemed like a similar mission, just on a much bigger scale.

I wished someone would do something to try to preserve Oaky Woods, and in the final analysis, I thought it might as well be me. The worst thing that could happen, after a lot of effort, is that I would fail. I am certainly a realist, but the preservation of Oaky Woods was too important an issue not to mount a concentrated effort to save the land from development. At that point in time, it appeared that our conservation cause was already lost, and we were down 6 to nothing in the 7th inning! But you never know how the game is going to end.

I had hunted, hiked and enjoyed the land, along with thousands of others for many years, and I could not believe that it would disappear in my lifetime. I had worked on promoting the state's purchase of Oaky Woods since 1986 when I wrote the Sunday Outdoor Column for the Warner Robins Daily Sun Newspaper. That was a small part time gig that I was able to handle with my full -time job in Law enforcement.

Neil Herring, spokesman with the Sierra Club, does an TV interview at the Oaky Woods check station with John Trussell.

So, my involvement with this issue spans from 1986 to 2010 when the state finally made the purchase. That was a long time! That involvement included many tv and radio interviews, newspaper articles and speaking engagements. Just in case you are wondering, it was all a volunteer effort and I paid my own expenses. Also, in case you are wondering, I don't think I deserve any special credit for working to preserve Oaky Woods, as I am a strong believer in the concept of the citizen- soldier. That's a person who votes, supports and takes part in government in any way that he can as a citizen, educates himself on important issues and supports our military to keep our country strong. We should all do these things.

A private citizen can get a lot done if they are dedicated and work hard. I believe everyone should work for things they believe in as our present civilization is built upon the work and sacrifices of the preceding generations. It takes a certain maturity (yes, I'm getting old) to appreciate the work of previous citizens and family members to build our country from its beginning in 1607 when the first settlers came to Jamestown, Virginia. With some research, I've been able to join several genealogical societies such as Sons of the America Revolution, Huguenot Society, Jamestown Society, Sons and Daughters of the Pilgrims and others. I encourage you to explore your own roots and find your relatives that made this country strong!

I also realized that if you really appreciate something, it must be shared so others can appreciate it too. With that goal in mind, I conducted many public hikes into Oaky Woods for scouting groups, school kids and teachers and other groups, and still try to do an annual hike in February of each year. Check the website, www.saveoakywoods for more information. Thanks to my son Brandon Trussell, for building and maintaining the website and to granddaughter Analyssa Trussell for editing assistance. My wife Billie also was a tremendous help on many fronts!

I am very grateful that after I started the group, "Save Oaky Woods" in 2007, I had many public and private supporters who wanted to see the land used for conservation purposes to preserve its wildlife, rare plants and unique habitats. I formed a steering committee to develop policy and offer public support and those important individuals were **Bob Turner,** Chief Magistrate Judge, Houston County, Alex Morrow, attorney, **Scott Knowles,** President, Straight Arrow Archery Club, **Bobby Tuggle,** Tuggle & O'Neal Insurance, **Dr. Dan Fussel,** Internal medicine- retired, **Ed Varner** Attorney, **Brian Fobbus,** Ducks Unlimited volunteer, **Les Ager,** Regional Fisheries Biologist, Georgia Dept of Natural Resources (retired) , **Ken Grahl** Regional Game Biologist, Georgia Dept of Natural Resources (retired), **Stan Martin**

Warner Robins conservationist, **Ed McDowell** USAF (retired), naturalist, **Danny Hamsley,** Registered Forester, Weyerhaeuser Corporation, **Walt Wood** Warner Robins Conservationist, **Jim Harden** Houston County Health Dept, retired, **Raleigh Jackson** Bonaire Conservationist, **Grady Trussell** Manager, Houston County Water Treatment, **Stephen Hammack**, Archaeologist, **Larry Ross,** Manager, Oaky woods WMA (retired),**Dr. Bob Sargent** President, Georgia Ornithological Society and Wildlife Biologist, **Tom McElrath**, Chuck's Bait & Tackle, **Troy Windham,** Aartistik Taxidemy, **Art Christie** Administrator, Houston Medical Center (retired) and **Okefenokee Joe**, well known naturalist and song writer.

Many Thanks to Sam Stowe and the great staff at the Georgia Wildlife Federation, who donated a booth to the Save Oaky Woods volunteers during the Perry Great Outdoor Shows. We talked with many thousands of citizens about our project. The support of all these fine individuals was very much appreciated!

Another very important group that aided "Save Oaky Woods" by doing their jobs was the writers of the Macon Telegraph. They knew a battle was brewing over Oaky Woods and they sought out the appropriate stories so that the public could be informed of the issues involved. I would like to thank Macon Telegraph Editor Oby Brown and writers Wayne Crenshaw, S. Heather Duncan, Jennifer Burke, Ed Grisamore, Steve Elkins and Travis Fain for the articles they wrote to educate the public on the issues around Oaky Woods. Some of the fine stories these writers penned are refenced in this book. Thanks also to Thomas Thurman, Amateur Archaeologist, who accompanied this writer on a trek into Oaky Woods. Visit his excellent website at Georgiafossils.com

Alex Morrow, left, Pat Morrow, Billie Trussell, and Art Christie provided refreshments for members of the Board of Natural Resources on their visit to Oaky Woods during their deliberations on the purchase of the land.

I would also especially like to thank Pierre Howard, President of the

Georgia Conservancy and Will Wingate, their Legislative Director, for visiting Oaky Woods with me and giving their strong voices to the effort to preserve this valuable property. Many thanks also to Neil Herring, Spokesman of the Sierra club and Lorra Lynch Jones, with WMAZ and Channels 24 and 41 for their interviews with me and coverage of Oaky Woods topics. I really appreciated Tom Williams, at Best Hardware Store in Bonaire, and others, for helping to sell our "Save Oaky Woods" bumper stickers.

When I started the effort to save Oaky Woods, the economy was going strong and no one saw the coming housing market collapse, caused by credit that was much too easy to obtain, with money borrowed by people who could not repay loans. When the financial bleeding slowed down, it left many banks and financial markets in shambles and the housing market came to a grinding halt. By 2008, the effort to "Save Oaky Woods" as a conservation project began to look better and better to the owners who were unable to advance their plans for a massive housing project due to the very tight credit market and conflicts with other local governments about the delivery of services to the development.

Save Oaky Woods Volunteers Robbie Russell, left, and Alex Morrow staff the organization booth at the Georgia Wildlife Federation's "Great Outdoor Show" in Perry in 2008. The show helped us build strong public support for the preservation of Oaky Woods

The owners of Oaky Woods Properties were Charles Ayers, Charlie McGlamery, Scott Free and A. L. Williams. I know Ayers, McGlamery, and Free on a casual basis and know them to be smart business men who negotiated with the state in good faith. Ayers, who was the principle negotiator, and I talked on a frequent basis and I always found him to be forthright and willing to share important information. He was under no obligation to talk with me about Oaky Woods, but he did, and for that I was thankful. Our cooperation led to productive discussions which, in some small part, led to a successful deal. All through our public relations campaign to save Oaky Woods, we maintained a positive attitude toward all individuals involved in the deal and we will always continue to do so.

There is an abundance of political points of view about Oaky Woods on the internet and we won't get into those issues here, other than reference some of the news articles, to preserve the historical record. I did try to get the Houston County Commissioners to let the voters of Houston County vote on a penny sales tax referendum or a bond issue to purchase a large portion of Oaky Woods, but no action was taken on the proposal. But at the time the economy was in a recession, which didn't help! It probably would have cost the average tax payer 20 per year and all the feedback I got on the issue was very positive, so I think it would have easily passed.

Okefenokee Joe, 2nd from right, a well-known singer and naturalist and Save Oaky Woods Advisory Board Member, receives a plaque of appreciation from John Trussell for his assistance with our effort during a meeting at the Warner Robins Air Force Museum of Aviation. Left is Stephen Hammock and far right is Alex Morrow

I do think that Governor Perdue missed a good opportunity to partner with Pierre Howard, President of Georgia Conservancy, to purchase Oaky Woods early in the process with little to no risk to the state. But with that missed opportunity, I do give Governor Perdue much credit for correcting the situation and putting 28.5 million in the state budget so a large portion, 10,015 acres of Oaky Woods, could be purchased in 2010. It wasn't long after that action was taken to purchase Oaky Woods, that I saw Governor Perdue in the Office Depot store in Warner Robins.

I thanked him for his efforts to fund the purchase of Oaky Woods and he said it was the right thing to do, and I could not have agreed more!

During his term, Governor Perdue was very supportive of outdoors issues and helped to set up and fund the Go Fish Education Center in Perry and Flat Creek Public Fishing area, just south of Perry. He also worked with the Georgia DNR to improve boating access to many large reservoirs around the state, so he has proven himself to be a friend of the outdoorsman. During Governor Perdue's term, I worked with the Georgia DNR on the Land Search Committee for the Flat Creek Public Fishing Area and on the Advisory Council for the Go Fish Center, both of which are now huge outdoor successes in Middle Georgia.

Senator Ross Tolleson, left, Les Ager, retired DNR Fisheries Supervisor and Governor Sonny Perdue worked together to plan, fund and implement important Georgia Outdoor projects. Next to Governor Perdue is Forest Ager.

As you read this book, you'll notice it is written in several sections. The first part is about the early history of Oaky Woods, its native American population and the coming of the Europeans. Next, we look at our native black bear population, wild Russian boars, cougars, wild jungle fowl and other wildlife that makes Oaky Woods Special! For many years, the funds provided by outdoorsmen provided the state the monies to lease the land for hunting and fishing, so of course there are a few hunting stories! Then we'll look at the Geologic history of middle

Georgia which includes discussions about our area being cover by the ocean, the coming of the last ice age, the woolly mammoths and other large creatures that walked in middle Georgia. Lastly, we will look at some special plants and animals in Oaky Woods.

I sincerely hope you enjoy this book and I hope to see you in Oaky Woods soon! This is your land now, so I trust that you will use it wisely and protect it for future generations!

CHAPTER 1

OAKY WOODS IN THE BEGINNING

A treaty was signed with the Indians in 1821, and Houston County was created by an act of the state legislature. Prior to then, this was Indian country and native Americans had lived and died on the land for 17,000 years. A clovis point dating from 13,000 years ago was found in Oaky Woods in 1967. The ground underneath the South field and The Bluff at Riverbend subdivisions, along Thompson Mill Road, and Oaky Woods, was inhabited for thousands of years by native Americans. They hunted large mammals like woolly mammoths, giant ground sloths and bison in Middle Georgia that disappeared due to a warming climate. I have found numerous Indian artifacts near Thompson Mill Road, including a Bolen Bevel point from 8,000 BC, making it 10,000 years old. Also found was a Kirk Corner Notch point, dating from 7,000 BC, making it 9,000 years old. Also found in this area were Indian pottery of the Swift Creek style, dating from 20 BC to 800 AD and pieces of soap stone bowls, dating to the same era, or earlier. Soap stone is steatite rock, which is a talc-schist type of metamorphic rock, found in north Georgia, so it was a trade item to middle Georgia Indians. It is soft and was carved into cooking bowls.

Indians from Oaky Woods often visited the Earth Lodge in Macon, which dates from 1015 AD.

The huge Indian Mississippian culture (800 AD to 1600 AD) that existed around the Ocmulgee National Monuments in Macon spread across Georgia and Indians from Houston County could travel by canoe or foot trails to the ceremonial mounds in Macon. The Ocmulgee River, which runs along the border of Oaky Woods, was the interstate 75 of its day, with large volumes of trade going down to Florida and northward to north Georgia and beyond. Indians hunted the forests, fished the river and plowed the ground here to plant beans, squash, potatoes and corn.

This Kirk Corner Notch Indian Point was found by author on private land near Thompson Mill Road, near Oaky Woods and dates from 7,000 BC, thus it is 9,000 years old!

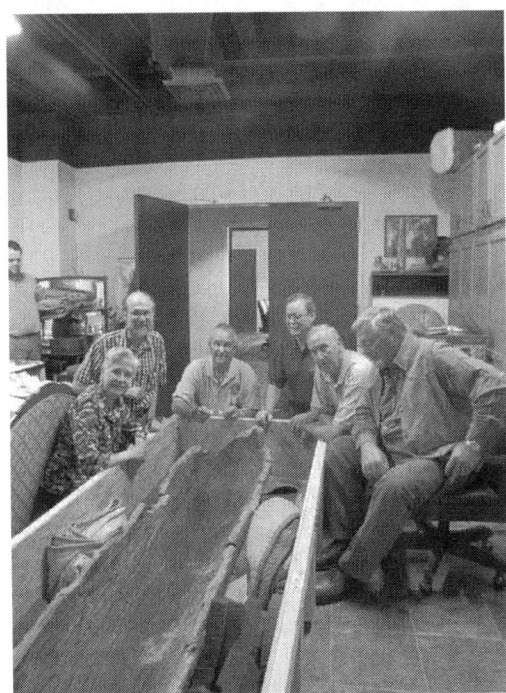

Native Americans traveled on the Ocmulgee, Oconee and other Rivers with dugout canoes. This one, in a padded box, was found preserved in river mud and is now in " Georgia's Old Capital Museum at the Depot" in Milledgeville. Members of the Ocmulgee Archaeological Society inspect the canoe. Visit the Museum!

During the settlement period, the numbers of native Americans had been greatly reduced by European diseases to which they had no immunity. It has been estimated by archaeologists that as many as 90 percent of native Americans were killed by smallpox, measles, chicken pox, influenza, and other diseases during the early colonization period. Of the Indians who survived and remained, many moved into Alabama territory or Florida to get away from white settlers, thus much of the land was sparsely inhabited.

Native Americans left a lot of artifacts in central Georgia. Jack Trussell found this 3,000-year-old Savannah River point at International Golf Club in Warner Robins

The Indians that remained were moved to Oklahoma in 1831-1838 in what is known as the trail of tears, while a few escaped to join the Seminoles in Florida. Approximately 46,000 Indians were removed from the Southeast region during this time.

An Indian soapstone smoking pipe that was found near the Ocmulgee river. It was a trade item from north Georgia as no soapstone exists in central Georgia

These pieces of Lamar Complicated Stamped Pottery date from 1350-1600 AD and were found near Sandy Run Creek in Houston County in 1962 by the author after he was inspired by a school trip to the Ocmulgee Indian Mounds in Macon. Thanks to all teachers for inspiring students! Take your family to the Mounds!

    The huge tract of land in southeast Houston County that would become Oaky Woods was settled by individuals who placed their names in land lotteries and got lucky with a fortunate draw. While some of the land in Oaky Woods was fertile and productive, the topsoil was rather thin and after a few years of farming it became eroded and depleted of nutrients. Fertilizers were unknown at the time, thus there was no quick way to improve the soil and farming could be a tough proposition. To complicate agriculture pursuits in Oaky Woods, the soil could have a high gumbo white clay content that dried and cracked in dry weather and turned into a thick quagmire when wet. The soil could also have a high limestone content many sedimentary rocks in it because eons ago it had been the at the bottom of the ocean.

From the late 1700's, Middle Georgia Indians often visited pioneer trading posts like this one at Fort Wilkerson, near Milledgeville, Georgia

    The Oaky Woods area was served by a stage coach line by in the mid to late 1800's and

Buzzards Roost, the stage coach depot, is listed on some old maps. Both Harvey Rackley and Bobby Tuggle think that the old house foundation and perimeter wall foundation for the old barn that served the stage coach horses still exsists, and I recentley visited the location to take some pictures with Bobby Tuggle. Old 1939 maps of Houston County show highway 127 ending at this location.

Bobby Tuggle, left, John Trussell and Brook Tuggle at the possible site of the Buzzard Roost stage coach stop, close to the Ocmulgee River on private property, near Oaky Woods. The old barn foundation for the stage coach horses is approximately 102 by 36 feet. Photo by Belinda Taylor

These early 1900-1915 coke bottles were found on private land near Oaky Woods. The left bottle is from Fort Valley, the right one from Macon. It is illegal to remove historical items from any state lands.

Next to the barn foundation, I found a coke bottle that dated to 1900-1915. The property was once in Oaky woods, but was sold off in the 1970's to a private individual. The old site is about 1/4 mile from the river and was also once served by a horse powered ferry that crossed the river to Twiggs County. For more information see "A Land so Dedicated- Houston County" by Bobbe Nelson in the Library. Other books you'll want to check out are " Running the River: Poleboats,

Steamboats and Timber Rafts on the Altamaha , Ocmulgee and Oconee" by Carlton Morison; Pioneer Days along the Ocmulgee by Russell Chalker; "A Wilderness still in the Cradle of Nature- Frontier Georgia"- Edward Cashin.

The author holds up a piece of stockade wall wood from the original 1806 Fort Hawkins. Soldiers at Fort Hawkins were in charge of "keeping the peace" on the Georgia frontier. The author was a volunteer amateur archaeologist working with the Lamar Institute that was researching and doing excavation work on Fort Hawkins in 2006. Visit and support Fort Hawkins!

This early American diner plate by J W Pankhurst was found by author in Crawford County and dates from the Mid- 1800's and was made in England. Similar wares have been found in Oaky Woods

By the time of the Civil War, cotton was the main cash crop and evidence of cotton farming can still be found in the forests today. Piles of sedimentary rocks can often be found along the edges of non-productive land. While today we might venture some mysterious origin of these rock piles, like Indian graves, the real nature of these rock piles is much more common. When farmers hit rocks with their mule drawn plow, they didn't want to hit the same rock again, so they would pick it up and move it to a spot where they would not be plowing.

Today the fields are gone and reverted to forests, but the rock piles still remain.

Back in 2001, I wrote a story in the Houston Home Journal about a beech tree carving that I had found in Oaky Woods, many years ago. The carving, shown below, displayed a man holding a moonshine jug in one hand and a cigar in the other hand. At the bottom, there was a carving of a bear paw and the date 1933. At the top of the carving was the name "Searcy" Jenkins. After that story appeared in the newspaper, I got a letter from Harvey Rackley, who was born in Oaky woods on March 30, 1927 and he knew Searcy Jenkins! Wow, I thought, what a discovery! Below are some of his memories, as relayed to this writer.

This 1933 carving was done by Searcy Jenkins and shows a man holding a moonshine jug and cigar. There is also a bear paw print on it. The tree, which is next to a creek near the North Road, died about 2012. Remnants of a moonshine still are close by, up the creek.

"When I was a baby, my grandfather William Rackley, was cutting sugar cane in a field in Oaky woods when he was bitten by a large rattle snake on September 11, 1927. He was bitten on the hand and it swelled up badly. They found a neighbor that had a Model T ford and tried to rush him to the doctor in Perry, but he died from the bite that same day".

Harvey Rackley recalled that several families lived in the Oaky Woods area and they were a tight group of people who often relied upon each other to get though the tough times, especially during the depression. He says that "nearly everything was raised on the farm, from vegetables, eggs, chickens, pigs and cows. They also hunted and fished for their food. All the deer had been hunted out, but there were plenty of small game, like squirrels, rabbits, quail, possum and raccoons to keep the dinner pot going. Trips to town were rare because we had little money, but looking back now, we really had all we really needed and didn't consider ourselves poor, which was good thing!"

Bobby Tuggle, Left, Brook Tuggle and John Trussell at the possible stage coach station foundation wall on private land near Oaky Woods.

He recalled the tree carver, Searcy Jenkins, as a close family friend. Searcy was the oldest of four kids and when his father died young, Searcy became the man of the house to look after his family. He worked on other nearby farms in Oaky woods but only earned 40 cents per day, which was good money at the time. The carving of the man holding the moonshine jug and cigar was a scene straight out of real life as the hard-working men would often retreat to the coolness of the small stream to clean up and refresh themselves with some home- made moonshine. The site is still in Oaky Woods, off North Road, but sadly the tree died many years ago. The picture you see here is all that remains of that precious tree.

This writer found the remains of the moonshine still a short distance up the stream from the tree carving and there were probably several other stills in the Oaky Woods area that got cranked up during the Prohibition era. Moonshining for was popular during prohibition days when the making of alcoholic beverages were illegal, which lasted from

1920- 1933. The Volstead Act, the prohibition law, was passed and became law in 1920 (the 18th amendment) and was revoked (the 21st amendment) by President Franklin D Roosevelt in 1933. Some may remember the popular TV show "The Untouchables", which aired from 1959-1963, which starred Robert Stack as Eliot Ness, the Federal Agent, who could not be bribed. While federal agents were chasing gangster Al Capone in Chicago, quiet farmers made their own home brew in Oaky Woods. Our "A Walk in Oaky Woods" winter tour will take you to an old moonshine still site.

Oaky Woods hikers gather at the old Moonshine still. The big steel container had its top blown off by federal Revenue agents. The top is lying across Big Grocery Creek. Please don't disturb the artifacts!

After all the residents moved out of Oaky Woods after World War two, when most of the land was bought by timber companies, there was no need for running water or electricity because no one lived there anymore! Most of the people left because farming the poor soil was unproductive and many men joined the World War Two effort. Jobs also became available during the war in the near- by cities. Another big factor was that electricity spread across Georgia in the late 1930' and 40's, but it wasn't available in Oaky Woods. This because there were not enough people in the area to justify the expense of running the power lines. If you wanted power, you needed to live in the cities or close to them.

Several old cemeteries are left in the Oaky Woods area and one of the easiest to find is the Smith Cemetery, also known as the Thompson cemetery.

To find it from Bonaire, Georgia, take Georgia Highway 96 East to Thompson Mill Road. Turn right on Thompson Mill Road, proceed approximately two (2) miles to Hiawassee Drive and turn left onto Hiawassee Drive. Proceed for about 1/2 mile and the cemetery is on the left a few yards off the road. This cemetery was originally surveyed by Addie P. Howell in 1977 and was included in her book "Cemeteries &

Obituaries of Houston County Georgia, 1982, as the "Thompson

Cemetery." The cemetery became known as the Thompson Cemetery during the 1900's after the land became the property of Mattie and Charlie H. Thompson, the heirs of Garrett Smith, son of William Smith, Jr.

The cemetery is the family burial site for William Smith, Jr. and his family, located on the original homeplace. William Smith, Jr. moved from Washington County, Georgia in the 1820's and established a large plantation on several hundred acres of land that he purchased near the Ocmulgee River. This land had been inhabited for thousands of years by native Americans. By the 1840's, William set aside this land for the family cemetery as his family members began dying. The cemetery was used by descendants of the William SMITH, Jr. family for the next century. A final survey of gravesites was completed by Ms. Sandra Morton on 27 December 2009.

A major cleanup of the Smith Family Cemetery was initiated on November 21, 2010 and on December 11, 2010 a group of resident volunteers completed the clearing of all brush and overgrowth of the cemetery. One of the graves is Abner Flewellen Redding, who was killed at the battle of Griswoldville, in Jones County on November 22, 1864, during the Civil War. Redding is unfortunate to have died in the war, but fortunate to have a nice headstone, which reveals the love of his survivors. It reads," Asleep in Jesus, blessed sleep. From which none ever wakes to weep. A calm and undisturbed repose, unbroken by the last of foes." (See grave marker , previous page.)

Billie Trussell points to the location of the Thompson Grist Mill that washed out in a flood many years ago.

Thompson Mill Road still bears the name of this pioneer family that ran a grist mill on Beaver dam creek, now on the south end of Thompson Mill Road. According to Harvey Rackley, the mill was run by Mitchell Perdue, born in 1848. Mitchell Perdue is Governor Sonny Perdue's Great uncle. He was Sonny's grandfather's brother. He lived in a one room house near the creek and ran the grist mill, making corn meal on a nearly daily basis.

Mitchell Perdue took a lot of his meals at the Walker's house, a nearby neighbor, and one day he failed to show up for breakfast. They went to check on him and he had died during the night, sometime in 1921, according to Rackley. The mill was gone by 1930, and was probably washed out by a flood, but portions of the dam still remain today. Thompson Mill Road used to run across the creek and into Oaky Woods, but sometime in the 1990's the road washed out and the County declined to fix it and let the road revert back to a natural state. I hope that someday the county will repair the road, as it would be a great access into Oaky Woods for the thousands of people that now live in that area.

As people moved away in the 1930's-40s, the land was purchased by the big timber companies. Wild game populations were very low due to unregulated hunting, as people hunted and fished to supplement their diets. Later, the realization that game laws were necessary to preserve game populations, led to the support of the re-introduction of deer and wild turkey into the Middle Georgia area. The Georgia DNR restocked 22 deer in 1962 into Houston County, a few miles east of Kathleen, into what would become Oaky Woods. These deer, from Wisconsin, who lived in a northern climate, were known for bigger body size and impressive antlers. In 1964, 6 deer from Jekyll Island were stocked into the Haynesville area. In 1965, 20 deer were stocked across the Ocmulgee River in Twiggs County, according to Georgia DNR records, compiled by Wildlife Biologist Supervisor Dick Whittington, of Fort Valley, who managed much of the restocking effort.

Wild turkey was restocked in the 1970's. Pigs were roaming wild in the Ocmulgee River Swamp from pioneer days and a very few black bears were holding on to their existence in the swamp, away from human influence. The abandoned farm land was planted in pine trees and it became a Wildlife Management Area in 1966, the land leased from the big timber companies.

In the early 1970's, about 100 wild red Jungle Fowl from Vietnam were stocked into Oaky Woods to see if they could survive here, says Dick Whittington, former DNR manager. But the Jungle Fowl could not adjust to our cold winters and hungry predators. I saw a Jungle Fowl while hunting in 1974 and that's the only one I ever spotted! You can still see these wild birds roaming the streets in Fitzgerald, Georgia or Key West, Florida.

Funds to support Wildlife Management Areas came from taxes on outdoor sporting equipment through the Pittman- Roberson Fund. Now State of Georgia owned since 2010, hopefully Oaky Woods will remain in a wild state forever for all citizens to enjoy! Some of the GPS site locations for future referenced are below. Remember that archeological artifacts cannot be removed from state lands and please protect all-natural areas!

1) Sand Dollar Cliffs: 32~27'58.03N, 83~33'35.36 W

2) Moonshine Still:32~27'50.86N, 83~33'16.54W

3) Ram Pump:32~29'17.73, 83~32'36.59

4) Black Prairie area:32~28"10.53 83~33"35.34W- There are several hundred acres.

Back in the 1970's Red Jungle Fowl from Asia where stocked in Oaky Woods but did not survive- but we still have this sign!

CHAPTER 2
THE STATE SHOULD BUY OAKY WOODS!

From the time Oaky Woods became a Wildlife Management Area back in 1966, politicians and a few outdoor guys like me promoted the idea that the state of Georgia should buy the land for the public good. The property was bought and sold several times and I feared that the state would lose the opportunity to lease the land as a Wildlife Management area. The only way to control the land was to buy it. At the time, I wrote the Sunday Outdoor column for the Daily Sun Newspaper that was a one story per week part time gig that I did with my full-time job in law enforcement. I wrote several articles about Oaky woods over the years, back in the 1980's-90's. I discussed the idea with numerous people, including State Representative Jay Walker, State Representative Larry Walker and my friend and newspaper writer, Steve Elkins.

He wrote a story about the issue entitled, "The State may buy Wildlife Area in Mid-State" that appeared on August 7, 1992. Yes, the first push to buy Oaky Woods occurred in 1992, as described in this article, but the effort fizzled out due to inaction by the state.
Elkins wrote that "State Rep. Jay Walker said that chances are "excellent that the state would buy the wildlife area. "We don't have a State Park in Central Georgia, we are underserved" (So, from 1992 to 2010, when the state finally purchased a portion of Oaky Woods, a period of 18 years elapsed!").

Area politicians had been pressing the Georgia Department of Natural Resources to purchase the land, which Procter & Gamble Cellulose Corp. was trying to sell. Walker said that if the State buys the land, it will be turned into a state park.

Elkins reported that State Rep. Larry Walker of Perry has also been working to get the state to purchase the land. He would like to see the area fall under Gov. Zell Miller's Preservation 2000 plan. But, Larry Walker said the move to buy the land has been a slow process.

"It gets on the front burner, then it's moved to the back burner. Then it's on the front burner again and then it's on the back burner again," He said.

Harvey Young, then the executive assistant to the director of the state Game and Fish Division, said Oaky Woods "looks to be" one of the 40 to 45 sites that will be studied further for possible inclusion in Preservation 2000.

A king snake in Oaky Woods

State Rep. Larry Walker of Perry has also been working to get the state to purchase the land. He would like to see the area fall under Gov. Zell Miller's Preservation 2000 plan. But, Larry Walker said the move to buy the land has been a slow process.

"It gets on the front burner, then it's moved to the back burner. Then it's on the front burner again and then it's on the back burner again." He said.

Harvey Young, executive assistant to the director of the state Game and Fish Division, said Oaky Woods "looks to be" one of the 40 to 45 sites that will be studied further for possible inclusion in Preservation 2000.

But after a lot of noise, nothing happened, and the state dropped the ball!

I was quoted in the story "John Trussell, an outdoors writer who has been active in trying to get the state to buy the land, said the area was once an ancient sea bed. Cotton plantations and a small community called Buzzard's Roost flourished there during the 1800s. The Old Hawkinsville Road ran right through it.

An alligator waits in the Ocmulgee River, near the mouth of Big Grocery Creek in Oaky Woods for some food to wander by.

Elkins interview with me continued, "Trussell said that Big Grocery Creek, which is located in the middle of Oaky Woods, was identified as a potential public fishing site by the State Department of Natural Resources. Oaky Woods contained 22,000 acres in the late 1960s, but some of the land was sold, including the area that fronts the Ocmulgee River.

"It's been shrinking over the years," Trussell said. 'And there are subdivisions being built close to it." Trussell said Oaky Woods and Ocmulgee Wildlife Management Areas are two of only a few habitats for bears in Georgia. The Ocmulgee WMA is across the Ocmulgee River from Oaky Woods in Twiggs, Bleckley, and Pulaski counties.

I told Elkins that the only other places in the state that wild bears can be found are the north Georgia mountains, the Okefenokee Swamp, and a very few in Bond Swamp.

Things rocked along for several years, then in 2004, the Weyerhaeuser Company, who owned the land at the time and leased it to the state, decided to sell all their Georgia timberlands, which was 322,615 acres. Undoubtedly, it was the largest transfer of private property in Georgia's recent history. The total land sold in Houston County was 33,817 acres, which included much of Oaky Woods. The Georgia Department of Natural Resources had Oaky Woods listed as their top priority for purchase as a "legacy Tract". But when the Nature Conscrvancy of Georgia, led by Chairman of the Board Pierre Howard, a former Lt Governor of Georgia, offered to loan the state the necessary funds, with no time table to pay back the money, Governor Sonny Perdue and DNR Commissioner Lonice Barrett, refused the offer, saying that the state could not afford the deal.

Soon the land went on the market and it was purchased by business men Charles Ayers, Charlie McGlamery, Scott Free and A. L. Williams who planned to put up to 30,000 homes on the land. But was the state still interested in buying the land for conservation?

Newspaper writer Shannon McCaffery wrote an associated press story on January 28, 2007, entitled "State's Oaky Woods Purchase Remains Up in the Air" that weighted the many issues surrounding Oaky Woods. McCaffery wrote, "From a logging road overlooking the Oaky Woods Wildlife Management Area, pine trees and hardwoods draped with honeysuckle vines stretch to the horizon.

McCafferty wrote, "John Trussell gestures down to where Big Grocery Creek - barely visible - cuts through the woods.

"That's where the bears gather," said Trussell, of Warner Robins. "And that's also where they want to develop."

McCafferty reported that plans to build up to 35,000 homes in the cradle of this popular hunting and recreation area have riled this middle Georgia community. Under Perdue's watch, the state declined to bid on Oaky Woods when timber giant Weyerhaeuser put the 20,000-acre tract on the auction block in 2004.

Under Perdue's watch, the state declined to bid on Oaky Woods when timber giant Weyerhaeuser put the 20,000-acre tract on the auction block in 2004.

McCafferty reported that letting Oaky Woods go was a colossal missed opportunity, claim some local residents. And Sonny - as most everyone here still calls the governor - should have known better. The land literally sits in his back yard. Perdue argues that the state didn't have the money at the time and that he still would like to preserve Oaky Woods, which is where he learned to hunt.

John Trussell, far left,, leads a group of hikers through Oaky Woods

The new owners of Oaky Woods said they still are willing to sell if the state is willing to pay their asking price. At the time in 2007, a spokeswoman for the Department of Natural Resources said officials remain interested in Oaky Woods, which is one of six priority areas in the state. Beth Brown said any purchase likely would require a partnership of some kind. "The state should not be looked upon as a sole source for funds," she said. This writer spoke to several Houston County Commissioners about a bond issue to raise money for the Oaky Woods, but the idea never got any traction. Still, residents were hoping Perdue somehow would come through for them.

McCafferty wrote that "Trussell, an environmental enthusiast and hunter, said building in Oaky Woods is like building homes along the edge of the Grand Canyon. "You just don't do that," as I was quoted. But the stalemate continued.

Things rocked along, then a miracle of sorts happened! I admit I don't pray nearly as often as I should, but I was surely hoping for a miracle to help us preserve Oaky Woods. Then it happened in a quiet manner as my prayer was partly answered!

It all happened on one of my many free public hikes, this one with a group of boy scouts. A scout leader picked up a rock during the hike and back at the truck I was amazed that she had found a whale bone vertebra! I reported the find to my friend and writer, Wayne Crenshaw at the Macon Telegraph and he penned a story, "Whale of a Find- Oaky

Woods Backers Cite Fossil Discovery", that appeared late 2007. Here are a few quotes from that article.

Crenshaw wrote, "John Trussell has spent 31 years looking for a whale bone in the Oaky Woods wilderness in Houston County, but Amanda Rhonemus found one on her first visit.

Trussell didn't seem to mind, though, that Rhonemus made the discovery while Trussell was giving her Cub Scout Pack a tour of the wildlife management area on Wednesday.

"To find one on top of the ground in a whole piece is fairly rare," said Trussell, who is involved with a group trying to save Oaky Woods from development. "It's pretty exciting." Crenshaw reported that Rhonemus, a Webelos patrol leader, picked up the object thinking it might be an Indian artifact, possibly an ax head. When she showed it to Trussell, he immediately recognized it as the vertebra of a prehistoric whale. To be sure, he consulted Thomas Thurman, a local amateur paleontologist, and Thurman agreed. They e-mailed photos to Dr. Jonathan Geisler, curator of paleontology at the Georgia Southern Museum and he confirmed it.

Crenshaw reported "It's easy to find fossilized sand dollars and sea shells on the property, Trussell said, if you look in the right locations, but he has been looking for a whale bone on the site since he was 15 and had no luck."

I had been giving free tours of Oaky Woods to try to generate public interest in saving it. I was giving a tour to Webelo Pack 566 of Warner Robins when Rhonemus found the whale bone.

"After Trussell identified it, she offered to give it to him. But even though he had been looking for a whale bone for most of his life, he told her she should keep it."

Contacted later by Crenshaw, Rhonemus said "she has loaned the fossil to her son's school, Shirley Hills Elementary, where it is currently on display in the library. "I thought it would be a great teaching tool. The kids were excited about it. "She added she had never heard of Oaky Woods previously. "I think it's kind of sad they are wanting to develop it because there are such neat things like that out there," she said.

Crenshaw reported that "Trussell said it appeared to be the vertebra of a basilosaurus whale, probably about 32 million years old. The whale averaged about 60 feet in length. For Trussell, the find is ammunition for his case that Oaky Woods is a place worth saving. Currently leased to the state as a wildlife management area, the 20,000-acre woods south of Bonaire is privately owned and slated to become a housing development."

Oaky Woods is home to a large variety of wild animals. Deer track at top, wild turkey track at bottom

Public interest in Oaky Woods remained strong and Crenshaw wrote another story entitled, "New Hope for Oaky Woods", on January 20, 2008. Crenshaw wrote "A year ago, John Trussell didn't have a lot of hope that Oaky Woods Wildlife Management Area, where he has hunted since he was 15, could be saved from development. But now he thinks things have changed.

The political climate has improved, the state is in better financial shape and a slowing housing market might make owners of the 20,000-acre tract more willing to sell it," Trussell said.

I also wondered how many people will actually want to live in an area where black bears might become backyard visitors.

And perhaps most encouraging was a recent example of how the commitment of local residents can spur the state to invest in land preservation.'

In late 2007, Gov. Sonny Perdue announced the $45.8 million purchase of 6,865 acres for the Paulding Forest Wildlife Management Area. Like Oaky Woods, the property had previously been leased by the state. The purchase deal included $15 million that Paulding County raised through a bond referendum in which voters, by a 2-1 ratio, agreed to a property tax increase to fund acquisition of the land.

Crenshaw reported "Trussell thinks the same thing could happen in Houston County with Oaky Woods. He is heading a group called Save Oaky Woods that aims for a similar deal".

"The group has a Web site, www.saveoakywoods.com, and it is selling bumper stickers to raise money for the cause. It's the first organized effort to save the popular nature area, which has been open to the public for more than three decades."

"Trussell said he believes voters would support a bond referendum. The key is to make it affordable to the average person," he said.

The Paulding County deal included $15.2 million from the Georgia Land Conservation Program, $7.7 million in federal funds and $7.8 million from private foundations and conservation organizations.

Crenshaw reported that the Paulding referendum called for up to 1 mill in additional taxes each year for 20 years, said county clerk Beverly Cochran, but that could fluctuate depending on other factors, such as residential growth. In fact, she said, in 2007 the tax rate is not going up at all. The county also estimates that land deal would cost the owner of a $200,000 home less than $23 per year.

At that point in time it was unknown what a similar deal might look like in Houston County. The cost could not be determined until an agreement is reached on a price. Federal, state and private contributions would also have to be factored in before calculating how much Houston County taxpayers would need to kick in to preserve Oaky Woods.

Crenshaw reported that "Houston County Commission Chairman Ned Sanders said there have been no formal talks about calling for a bond referendum, but he said he intends to explore the idea."

Hikers with John Trussell at the Big Red Oak called the "Oaky Woods Sequoia"

Unfortunately, the bond issue never got any support from political leaders in Houston County, so voters never had the chance to vote on the matter. (But in the end, it was a moot point as Governor Perdue thankfully acted at the end of his term to put monies in the states conservation budget to address the issue).

But by 2009 the recession had hit the housing market hard and all financial institutions were taking a licking. The owners of Oaky Woods decided to explore selling the land to conservation interests. Travis Fain, another writer for the Macon Telegraph, wrote a story, "Lobbyist hired to sell Oaky Woods as Nature Preserve" on January 23, 2009.

He reported that "The group that owns Oaky Woods, a massive tract of prime woodland in Houston County, has hired a lobbyist in another push to sell the land as a permanent nature preserve.

The group, which includes several Houston County businessmen, hired Brad Alexander Lt. Gov. Casey Cagle's chief of staff until last year when he left to form a new lobbying and consulting group, Georgia 360 LLC. Alexander said he's working with several entities in the hopes that funding for the deal can be split up. John Trussell, who founded Save Oaky Woods, said money could be stitched together from public and private sources. That could include a penny sales tax in Houston County, he said."

Fain reported "Trussell said he talked to Ayer recently about the plan and that Ayer said the ownership group won't raise the price it charges the state to lease the land as a wildlife management area next year. As a sign of goodwill, Trussell said."
During the process, the Oaky Woods owners sought a zoning change in connection with their development plans. They were exploring the possibility of a private development.

The group, which then called itself Winding River Development, applied for a variance that would allow for construction of a wastewater treatment plant on 18 acres of the property. County officials determined the request would require a regional impact study by the Middle Georgia Regional Development Center. It was determined that the planned development was in the city of Warner Robins service area and that halted the private development idea. Mayor Donald walker said it was a dead issue and he couldn't support it.

This position from the city of Warner Robins caused the owners of Oaky Woods to withdraw their application for a zoning variance. This subject was covered by the story "Oaky Woods Development Plan Halted" by Jennifer Burke in the Macon Telegraph on December 4, 2009.

In her interview with me she stated, "John Trussell, founder of Save Oaky Woods, said the best use for the property is a wildlife management area. The withdrawal of the two applications is good news, at least in the short term, he said.

A pair of Cherokee Roses, the official Georgia State Flower, in Oaky Woods

"Probably construction of a massive subdivision is not imminent at the present time," he said. "It does not mean it cannot happen in the future."

His organization recently

received nonprofit status, which will make it easier to solicit funds and apply for grants to study the area, he said."

About that time, I gave a tour of the property to Pierre Howard, president of the Georgia Conservancy. As a result, the group renewed its call for preservation.

"We feel (Oaky Woods) is a state treasure because of the location, because of the multiple uses it can be put to by the people who live in that area and people all over the state. It's a primary place for sportsmen," Howard said. In addition, "the natural value of the property is rare."

Burke reported that Howard, a former lieutenant governor who was named to the group's top post earlier that year, said the Georgia Conservancy plans to lobby legislators when the General Assembly convenes. "Some of those things like Oaky Woods, you can lose the opportunity to preserve them," he said. "I think this will be Gov. (Sonny) Perdue's last chance to save that property for future generations of Georgians."

THE PENDING BUY: In late 2010, the state finally got ready to buy Oaky Woods and the owners were ready to finally sell. Joe Kovak, Jr, a writer for the Macon Telegraph, wrote a story "State may buy large part of Oaky Woods" on November 30, 2010 that stated, "More than half of the Oaky Woods Wildlife Management Area in Houston County that's now leased by the state from private owners could soon become public land for good if Georgia officials agree to pay a nearly $29 million asking price".

In early December 2010, the state's purchase of thousands of acres of a popular Houston County wildlife management area cleared another significant hurdle Wednesday when the Department of Natural Resources board voted 11-6 to approve the $29 million deal. The story was covered by Macon Telegraph writer Heather Duncan in "Oaky Woods Deal Elicits Outrage, Enthusiasm, on December 9, 2010.

The state purchased 10,000 acres of Oaky Woods west of the Ocmulgee River, including black bear habitat, the highest quality known Georgia Eocene chalk prairies, endangered plants, and river habitat for rare and endangered fish and mussels. The 11-6 vote on the deal was much closer than the numbers might indicate.

In fact, on the morning of the vote, the majority of the Board were opposed to the deal. I had several conversations with Charles Ayer, the principle land owner negotiator that morning and it appeared the deal would not pass. We discussed the possibility of adding some additional land to the deal to get more river front land and the price per acre down a little, and that action on the part of the sellers sealed the deal to the benefit of all parties. I give Charles Ayer and the Georgia DNR Board credit for making the deal work as it was long, complicated process.

After the deal was done, Ayers made the following comments. "The state drew the lines they wanted. "They got most of the river frontage and most, if not all, of the creek bottoms," as well as the main road systems through the property."

And the state actually negotiated extra acreage and a better price in the last week, said Duncan. The original agreement would have included 9,595 acres for $3,000 an acre. The final price worked out to about 2,874 per acre.

"We wanted to make it work," Ayer said. "We've always wanted to conserve part of" the land.

Ayer and Perdue's spokesman said the governor was not involved in the negotiations. But the timing of the agreement, only a few weeks before the end of Perdue's term, lead some observers to credit the governor, wrote Duncan.

"I commend Sonny Perdue and the owners for reaching this compromise," said John Trussell, head of a citizens group called Save Oaky Woods. "I'm happy with what they did. It's been a long, hard process... The curtain was closing on this deal with the governor leaving office." As I said in the opening section of this book, I give Governor Sonny Perdue much credit for providing the essential state funds for the purchase of Oaky Woods. In the end, it was his leadership on this issue that got the deal done.

Duncan added, "Trussell, a Houston County naturalist who conducts tours of Oaky Woods, said most people he's heard from are pleased with the deal. "A few years ago, we were working hard and just hoping the state would take some positive action." He said he hopes to see Save Oaky Woods evolve into a Friends of Oaky Woods support group for fundraising and volunteering. "We're going to stick together and try to expand the perimeter where we can," he said.

The information above about the Oaky Woods land deal is just the essentials. My involvement with supporting the state's purchase of Oaky Woods spanned from 1992 to 2010- a period of 18 years and I must say it was worth it! You can still find abundant information about Oaky Woods from many web sources.

A buck is checking out a doe

CHAPTER 3

RUNNING WATER COMES TO OAKY WOODS

No electricity, no running water, all transportation and work were done by horses and mules – it's hard for us to imagine these living conditions on a daily basis during the pioneer days of Oaky Woods. But that's the situation during the 1800's to early 1900's in oaky Woods and all of rural Georgia. However, good things were being invented around the world and at least one homestead in Oaky Woods had running water, powered by a Hydraulic Ram Pump. It's a simple pump that uses the force of water running downhill to use valves and pressure to force water into a pipe to be transported to where it is needed.

This tree carving from September 3, 1912 was found on a beech tree near the Hydraulic Ram water pump. The tree was blown over by a storm.

I found the remains of the old pump system back in the early 1970's and wondered what it was until Harvey Rackley, a native of Perry, who was raised in Oaky Woods back in the early 1900's, told me about how the system worked. Harvey remembers the clanking sound the pump made while working and seeing the water being delivered to a house near- by. He thinks the water went to the home of Ruel Davidison, whose family still lives in central Georgia.

The first self-acting ram pump was invented by the Frenchman Joseph Michel Montgolfier (best known as a co-inventor of the hot air balloon) in 1796 for raising water in his paper mill at Voiron, France. His friend Matthew Boulton took out a British patent on his behalf in 1797. The first US patent was issued to Joseph Cerneau and Stephen S. Hallet (1755-1825) in 1809. US interest in hydraulic rams picked up around 1840, as further patents were issued, and domestic companies started offering ram pumps for sale. It is not known who owned the Oaky Woods hydraulic ram pump, but Ruel Davidson, an early Oaky Woods Pioneer, lived close by and his family still lives in the Bonaire area. Some of the Perdue family also lived around Oaky Woods, as did the Mills, Jenkins, Rackley families and several others. At the top of a small hill, there was a small spring head and a very small retaining pond to hold a supply of water. The water was drained off through a metal pipe and it ran downhill to the ram pump. I have hunted around this spring for many years and it has never run dry, even in times of drought.

I will try to simply explain how the pump worked. To use a ram pump, you must have a source of water situated *above* the pump. For example, you must have a pond on a hillside so that you can locate the pump below the pond. In Oaky Woods, they built a small reservoir of water by damming up a stream head on the side of a hill. Then a pipe was run down- hill from the pond to the pump. The pump has a valve that allows water to flow through this pipe and build up speed.

Once the water reaches its maximum speed, this valve slams shut.

As it slams shut, the flowing water develops a great deal of pressure in the pump because of its inertia, then the pressure forces open a second valve.

High-pressure water flows through the second valve to the delivery pipe (which usually has an air chamber to allow the delivery pipe to capture as much high-pressure water as possible during the impulse).

The pressure in the pump falls. The first valve re-opens to allow water to flow and build up momentum again. The second valve closes, then the cycle repeats.

The delivery pipe can rise some distance above both the pump and the source of the water. For example, if the pump is 10 feet below the pond, the delivery pipe might be up to 100 feet above the pump.

The one big disadvantage of a ram pump is that it wastes a lot of water, but that water could be used somewhere else. Typically, only about 10% of the water it consumes actually makes it up the delivery pipe. The rest flows out of the pump as the water builds momentum.

So, the folks in Oaky Woods, without electricity, tried to use emerging technology to make life easier. Next to the location of the Ram Pump was an old American beech tree with the date of 9/3/1912.

In 1912, the model T Ford was only four years old, the ship Titanic sank in April and the gilded Victorian era was well underway. Handle bar mustaches and lacey dresses were all the rage. Women had yet to gain the ability to vote, but the 19th amendment was passed in 1920 to correct that issue! The tree carving represents a brief moment, frozen in time.

The tree died around 2011, and I still have the tree carving preserved for educational use. Ram hydraulic pumps are still used around the world; Google the term for more information and you can see them in action on YouTube.

My Great grandmother Rosa Barton McDuffie pumps water in early 1900's

CHAPTER 4

BLACK BEARS IN OAKY WOODS

Note: This article discusses the early days of the central Georgia Bear hunt when a one- day hunt was held on both Oaky Woods and Ocmulgee WMA's. Later the hunt was moved to just Ocmulgee WMA, then in 2011 the hunt was moved to private lands in Houston, Twiggs and Bibb Counties. Written by author for Georgia Outdoor News, December 2007.

A recent study on the Middle Georgia black bear population, conducted by the Georgia Department of Natural Resources with the assistance of University of Georgia researcher Kacy Cook in cooperation with landowners, concluded June 30, 2007 with some very interesting results.

Three bear cubs found by wildlife biologists on Oaky Woods WMA in 2007.

Bobby Bond, a Senior Wildlife Biologist from the Fort Valley DNR office who assisted with the study, said that the total population is very low, with only approximately 300 bears in the isolated woodlands of Oaky Woods, Ocmulgee Wildlife Management Areas and along the Ocmulgee River Corridor. In the 1700's, prior to widespread farming and development, bears inhabited all of Georgia. But with continued human population growth, the bears were killed out and the survivors pushed into isolated, remote locations. Today the DNR estimates that 1,200 - 1,500 bears live in the rugged North Georgia Mountains, while 700-800 live around and in the Okefenokee Swamp, inhabiting ranges that are five times larger than the Central Georgia range. Of the three populations, the Central Georgia bears are in the most perilous situation due to loss of habitat and low population.

However, Bond says the present population is stable and may have slightly increased since the 1980's due to the protection of remote habitats on Oaky Woods and Ocmulgee WMAs. The protected boundaries for Central Georgia bears have diminished sharply since timber giant Weyerhaeuser's sell out in 2004. Previously, Georgia leased or owned 47,000 acres along the Ocmulgee River in Houston, Twiggs and Pulaski Counties, about 28,000 in Ocmulgee WMA and the remainder in Oaky Woods WMA. Since the sale, the state has lost 7,350 in Ocmulgee WMA and all the Oaky Woods tract was sold to private developers who plan to place up to 30,000 residential or commercial properties on the land. This would result in an approximately 50% decrease in habitat for the Middle Georgia bear population. This vast loss of habitat would be very detrimental to the bear population, says Raye Jones, Oaky Woods Manager and Wildlife Biologist Rashida Stanley, and could mean the total die-off of the Middle Georgia bear population in the foreseeable future.

In conducting the bear study, 84 bears were captured on Oaky Woods, Ocmulgee WMAs and nearby properties. Each bear was measured, weighed and aged. The average age of males was 4 years, while females were slightly older at 6 years. The average weight was 220 pounds for males, 130 pounds for females. Surprisingly, the annual home range for females was 3,600 acres, but for males it was 10 times larger at 41,600 acres. The largest bear weighed a whopping 460 pounds, but it was killed while crossing a road in south Houston County. Road mortality was the leading cause of death for the bears, with 10 road-killed bears reported in 2006, but the number could be higher. In 2005, there were 17 reported road-killed bears in Central Georgia with most fatalities occurring on GA Highway 96 from the Ocmulgee River the GA 129/87 Tarversville intersection then just a few miles north and south of that intersection along GA 129/87. Perhaps because the Middle Georgia bear population has less land to roam, the roadkill number is higher here than both the north and South Georgia population, according to Bond. One bear, says Bond, was a real long- distance traveler and went 31 miles into Wilcox County. But it was poached and left dead in the woods, illustrating the threat bears face when they travel away from the protected and isolated habitat of Oaky Woods and Ocmulgee WMA.

Adult black bear observed during the bear study on Oaky Woods WMA in 2007.

What lies ahead for Oaky Woods WMA and the bear population? Much is unsettled, but for now the owners continue to lease the property to the state for Wildlife Management Area use. Meanwhile they are proceeding ahead with plans for a very large residential and commercial development called "Winding River." They also have pending plans for a ground application sewage plant on land located near Kovac Road. Since a sewage plant is not allowed on rural-agricultural zoned land, their zoning appeals request will begin with the Zoning Appeals Board, who only have recommending authority on this issue, with final action being taken by the Houston County Commissioners. Although the owners request is pending, the actual date of the hearings before county officials is not yet set but expected very soon. The public is invited to attend these hearings and express opinions.

While the development plans on Oaky Woods are pending, there is still hope that all or major portions of the Oaky Woods WMA can be purchased for continued public outdoor recreational use. This writer spoke with Governor Sonny Perdue at the GON Outdoor Show in Macon in August and again in December and he expressed a positive attitude in stating that if Houston County officials can promote and pass a local bond issue it would certainly help leverage larger amounts of available state conservation funds and encouraged the effort. State Senator Ross Tolleson also stated that he would like to see the Houston County and the state purchase major portions or "sensitive areas" of the WMA. Recently the citizens of Paulding County, with a 70% "yes" approval vote, passed a 15 million- dollar bond issue to purchase 7,200 acres of Paulding WMA that were threatened by development. Their action will raise the tax on a 200,000 home by 23.40 per year, or less than 2.00 per month. This writer has discussed a bond issue, similar to the one passed in Paulding County with all the Houston County Commissioners and all express a desire to hear more information, but no official actions have taken place. This writer has also discussed the preservation and purchase of Oaky Woods with two members of the Governor's Land Conservation Council who reside in central Georgia. Both Chuck Levell, the well-known keyboard player for The Rolling Stones band who resides in Twiggs County and Dr. John Bembry, a veterinarian from Hawkinsville, said they would very much like to see a proposal to purchase Oaky Woods WMA to come before their board in an application for state funds. The Land Conservation Council was appropriated 42 million dollars for purchase of statewide conservation lands and 26 million from the Nature Conservancy may still be available if local and state officials can put together a viable proposal. But much remains to be resolved.

Will the owners continue to push ahead with development plans or will they agree to a reasonable appraisal price for the property and assist with public purchase of the property to ensure that this legacy tract remains intact for future generations? If the property is developed, Bond anticipates that the nuisance bear complaints will skyrocket up as it hard to imagine property owners using 30,000 bear proof trash cans and using good care in not leaving dog food and other food sources in their yards that will attract bears. Many questions remain, and the ending has not yet been written, but ultimately the bears will end up losing in the bear versus man struggle on Oaky Woods WMA if the land is developed.

In the meantime, a one- day bear hunt is scheduled for Ocmulgee WMA for December 15th, but no bear hunting is allowed on the Gum Swamp tract. In the past, a few hundred hunters have participated in these hunts and typically one bear has been harvested every other year, but no bears have been harvested since 2001. According to Kevin Kramer, Region Wildlife Biologist, the hunt allows bear hunters a limited opportunity to bag a bear without harming the resource and it helps to educate the public about Middle Georgia's unique bear population. The one- day hunt is only held on Ocmulgee WMA to help concentrate hunters and DNR staff on one tract while Oaky Woods has been maintained as a refuge for the bears. Hunters must check in at the Ocmulgee check station and are limited to one bear with a minimum weight of 75 pounds. Hunting success on this hunt is very low, usually about one percent and the last bear was harvested in 2001, but the hunt gives hunters a chance to participate in a special hunting experience and strengthens public support for a healthy bear population.

A bear at a supplemental feeder. In Georgia, it is illegal to hunt bears within 200 yards of a feeder.

CHAPTER 5
MIDDLE GEORGIA BEARS- HOW MANY?

How many bears are wandering in the forests of Oaky Woods and central Georgia? That's a good question and after several studies, we still don't have a firm answer. Obviously, there's no way to physically count the bears, so we rely on statistical analysis using mathematical models. This is known as Wildlife Management Science, but it's really just the best educated guess. Game Biologists sometimes refer to it as a swag, or "scientific wild assumptive guess" and the results achieved can be only as reliable as the data gathered and the statistical model used, but the methods improve as we move into the future. Many years ago, Region Wildlife Biologist Ken Grahl told me that using old fashion Wildlife Biological methods, he determined that there were approximately 300 bears in central Georgia, or about one bear per 900 acres of habitat.

Bears are very good at finding food. Here, a bear comes out on a steel cable to get to bird seed!

However, in 2015 after the three-year study had ended, University of Georgia Researchers concluded that we only had 140 bears in central Georgia (1). This was an especially concerning figure when an active annual hunting season was still in place for this very small bear population. The study, done by the University of Georgia's Warnell School of Forestry and Natural Resources, puts the population at 140. It had previously been estimated at about 300. Crenshaw reported that "John Trussell, a leading advocate for wise management of the bears, said the study results do not surprise him, and he believes the population estimate is accurate. He did not push for ending the annual hunt, but he said he hopes the state will be cautious with it and consider limiting the number of hunters through a quota system. "I think we have taken the surplus bears out," he said.

Bear and cub attracted to sardines during study

Crenshaw continued, "Trussell is a hunter and has killed bears, but he said due to the population estimate, he has made the personal decision not to participate in the annual hunt. He says that he would be glad to let other hunters, who have not taken a bear, to get one on the hunt. Bobby Bond, a senior wildlife biologist for the Georgia Department of Natural Resources, said the state had already thought the previous estimate was high when it started allowing the hunt. With the later hunting day having minimal impact on the population, he did not foresee any immediate change coming as a result of the study".

The previous estimate was too high, but the lower figure is also due to vehicle accidents and hunting, said Michael Chamberlain, PhD, a lead researcher. The new study is the most thorough and accurate one the state has done on the population, he said. It included an area south of Interstate 16 and down Ga. 96, then south to the Ocmulgee and Oaky Woods wildlife management areas.

The new study also looked at a smaller area, but that has been expanded and a few more bears may get added to the population. The state began allowing an annual one-day hunt in 2011, and that resulted in 34 bears being killed, which raised objections from wildlife advocates. The next year 14 were killed. Then in 2013 the state moved the date back to when bears were starting to den, and only one bear was killed. In a hunt held Dec. 13 five were killed, making a total of 54 lost from hunting.

However, soon after lower bear estimate was released, bear researcher Mike Hooker re-analyzed the same data, using different models and determined that we had 240 bears in central Georgia. In 2016 researcher Annaliese Ashley, working on her master's thesis, estimated that the bear population in central Georgia was 458.

A story in the Macon Telegraph, by Wayne Crenshaw, "More Bears than Thought in Middle Georgia?" (3), covered the new information. "Based on research by the University of Georgia, the state had previously estimated the bear population in Middle Georgia at 240. However, with a fresh look at the same data as well as including a larger area and an additional year of research, the population is now estimated at 458. Researchers reached that number using a model that estimates the number of bears in an area based on hair collected from snare traps. By calculating the probability, which is low, that a bear will leave a sample in the trap, researchers can use the number of samples collected to help determine the actual number of bears. DNA testing of the hairs is done to determine how many different samples are collected."

The estimate looked at a slightly larger 278,000-acre area mostly in Houston, Bleckley, Twiggs and Pulaski counties. It calculated about one bear per 625 acres in the area.(2)

Obviously, the bear population did not go from 140 to 458 in a short amount of time. That would be a 227% increase in two years and that didn't happen. The 2016 bear population estimate of 458 is based on a slightly larger area and a research model that was more liberal than the previous models, and researchers stated that it might be counting bears that don't exist.

Mike Hooker, aided by several DNR staff, collects DNA info from a bear at the check station

As stated earlier, it is difficult to count bears walking around in the woods and perhaps the latest estimate is overly optimistic. But hopefully new data and more DNA evidence in the future will increase our knowledge and our middle Georgia bear population will increase over time

Here, bears often claw and rub pine sap onto their fur.

The core area for central Georgia bears is centered on the Ocmulgee River, around Oaky Woods and Ocmulgee WMA's. There will be reports of bear sightings in Bond swamp and Piedmont Refuge in Jones County, and other counties, as young male bears expand their range. There are very few bears in the outlying fringe areas, but hopefully the population will grow and spread. The bottom line is we still don't know, and never will know, how many bears are in middle Georgia. Thus, there is still reason to carefully monitor this population and carefully control hunting opportunities.

Just to be clear, this Outdoor Writer strongly supports all types of hunting, including bear hunting, when it does no harm to the population. I have two bears hanging on my wall and really don't need another, but I'm happy for other hunters to hunt for middle Georgia bears. Like all hunting, it a great sport. Although I have been at times portrayed as a protector of the bears, especially in the quest to preserve Oaky woods, I was only advocating for wise bear management. If Oaky Woods had been developed, as planned, the small bear population would have been severely threatened and maybe wiped out in the long term. So, the small bear population became one of the main reasons I thought this land must be preserved. I placed bears on our posters and t-shirts, so the public could not miss our goals. Good stewardship dictates that "the thoughtful land stewardship you practice leaves a better world than you found for those who will follow". Hunters were the first conservationists and I believe this is the opinion shared by most hunters. We must insure that this bear population remains viable and healthy and grows, then we as hunters can enjoy some great bear hunts and the pleasure of seeing wild bears in our woods!

Here is Former Woody Woods Manager Raye Jones with two young bear cubs

    Most hunters I talk with are happy with the one- day season, but some hunters have wanted it to be expanded, claiming the bear population is growing. Bobby Bond said the GPS tracking in the study gives a good clue about why people may believe the bears population is higher. The bears move quite a bit, which leads to a lot of sightings, but there aren't really that many bears. Bears will often target baiting locations and stick very close to the area for as long as food is available, thus there are multiple sighting, often of the same bear.

When the first private lands bear season was started in 2011, 32 bears were killed and removed from the population, and many of the bears were females, which raised questions and concerns since bears are very slow to re-populate. That hunt removed approximately 10 percent of the middle Georgia bears from the population, the upper limit for a large normal population. But this was a small fragile population that could not sustain such loses. That high harvest looked especially troublesome when the population estimate was stated to be only 140 bears, thus the 32 bear loses could have a represented 23% of the total bears in middle Georgia, an unacceptable loss if the 140-population estimate was accurate.

The next year 14 bears were taken. In 2013 the state moved the hunt from November to December, when the female bears start to become less visible. That resulted in only one bear being taken, but it was a cold, rainy day. In 2014 just five bears were taken, but in 2016, 12 bears were taken, including nine females.

Small bear populations can also be stressed by population dynamic factors such as a lack of genetic diversity, lack of habitat and high deaths due to vehicle traffic volume and all three of these factors may be influencing the middle Georgia population. Thus, there is reason to carefully monitor this population.

We may also need to ask this question: Do we need to introduce bears with different DNA into the Oaky Woods population to diversify and strengthen their DNA? Kevin Kramer, Middle Georgia DNR Region Supervisor, says that is a possibility under consideration.

During the study, Dr Michael Chamberlain said that UGA researchers may be able to learn more about how the small size of the Middle Georgia bear population could affect its survival. Small populations have less genetic variation and can be more susceptible to declines in breeding or litter sizes, Chamberlain said.

"Isolated populations are also much more susceptible to a catastrophic change," he said. The DOT might fund a second phase in two or three years to track bear movements through the Ga. 96 underpasses, if they are built in the future. Currently the road expansion project is on hold. Another factor to consider is the low reproductive capacity of bears.

Left- Bears like to chew on and rub their backs on creosote poles.

While doe deer can reproduce at one year of age, bear sows won't normally reproduce until they are 3- 4 years of age. Even up until the 2017 one day bear season in Houston, Bibb and Twiggs Counties, the bear harvest was running up to 50% sow bears, which was unacceptable for this small population. Also, while deer bucks have antlers which helps hunters avoid shooting does when legally required, sow bear and male boar bears look alike, so every bear hunt ends up being an either sex bear hunt, thus extra precautions must be put in place. Sometimes bears are mistaken for wild pigs. It can happen like this:

A hunter shoots what he thinks is a wild pig and walks over to it, only to discover that he has illegally killed a bear. The hunter is faced with a moral dilemma, to turn himself in to law enforcement or walk away from the bear and hope he is not discovered. Unfortunately, I have found several dead bear carcasses in the woods over the years that were probably mistaken for wild hogs. The obvious answer to this problem is for hunters to be 100% sure of their target when they pull the trigger.

When the first bear hunt was held in 2011, baiting for deer was just allowed and the bear hunt was during the peak of the deer rut, which insured that the maximum number of hunters would be in the woods.

A story titled, "One Day Hunt kills 10% of Midstate Bears" by Heather Duncan, covered the hunt in the Macon Telegraph. "About a tenth of the Middle Georgia black bear population was killed when the first-ever open bear season was held in three Middle Georgia counties last month. Although some wildlife advocates are raising concerns about harm to the bear population, state officials say the hunt will be held the same way next year. Thirty-four bears were killed Nov. 12, half of them females, and all in an area near Tarversville in Twiggs County'. I stated in the story that I was concerned that too many female bears were killed, and that we should shift the hunt later in the year to protect sows bears.

I also stated, "It's taken us 100 years to get where we're at with the bear population. It's better to start slow."

Duncan reported that "Most of the bears were taken off a small area around Tarverville, in Twiggs County. "Anytime you get six bears on one property, that's a lot," DNR ranger Cpl. Robert Stillwell said.

Bears were using the deer bait, even though it was illegal to shoot bears within 200 yards of bait and several cases of hunting over bait were made. Unfortunately, several of the biggest bears taken during the hunts were confiscated by the DNR.

A large bear in a leg hold trap, waits to get fitted with a tracking collar

Later, the one-day season was moved to December, but still the bear sow kill rate was too high.

For the 2018 one-day bear season in central Georgia, the Georgia DNR wisely decided to move the hunt date into January when more sows would be more likely to be denned up with cubs and less likely to be harvested in the hunt. On that January 13, 2018 hunt, it was cold and windy, and two bears were taken, one male and one female. Although the hunting harvest was low, 17 bears were killed by road accidents and one mistaken for a wild pig and killed, thus 18 bears were lost to the population in 2017, plus the two hunting kills in January 2108. So, the total recent losses of 20 must be considered by the Georgia DNR.

Central Georgia bears do not normally hibernate through the winter, although they may retreat to dense cover for a short period of time during cold spells. I have spooked them out of thick brush piles on cold days. Time will tell if moving the hunts to a later and colder time in the year is an effective strategy to protect the sow bears.

Middle Georgia bears are part of WRD's five-year, $500,000 research study to try to estimate and monitor the middle Georgia bear population. Most of the cost for this study, which is taking place on Oaky Woods and Ocmulgee WMAs in Houston, Twiggs and Bleckley counties, is being paid for through Pittman-Robertson money, says Brad Gill, at Georgia Outdoor News. Part of that money is being used to allow University of Georgia students to spend long days and strange hours in the field to collect data monitoring the bears.

A large bear enters a bait station and the barbwire pulls some hair from which DNA can be determined.- Photo UGA

Kacy Cook is a UGA master's student in the School of Forest

Resources and was one of the students who started collecting bear telemetry data. Jeff Bewsher, Mike Hooker, Casey Gray, Annaliese Ashley, Dr Michael Chamberlain, UGA, John Bowers, Ga DNR, and Bobby Bond, Ga DNR, also contributed to the project. Also, thanks to Brad Gill at Georgia Outdoor News for his press coverage of this study.

According to Gill, although nothing is written in stone yet about how WRD should manage middle Georgia bears, there have been some interesting tidbits and some pretty unique findings to come from the first year of following these rambling bears. In fact, one such bear spent so much time rambling, it swam across Georgia's biggest reservoir and into another state.

"That was a unique behavior," said Kacy. "She was a 2-year-old female that was caught as a nuisance female in Gatlinburg, Tennessee. She was brought to the Tennessee/Georgia border and released in the Chattahoochee National Forest where there's plenty of bears and good bear habitat."

Home sweet home for a young female. Lifted from urbanization and put into the back hills of Georgia — what could have been better?

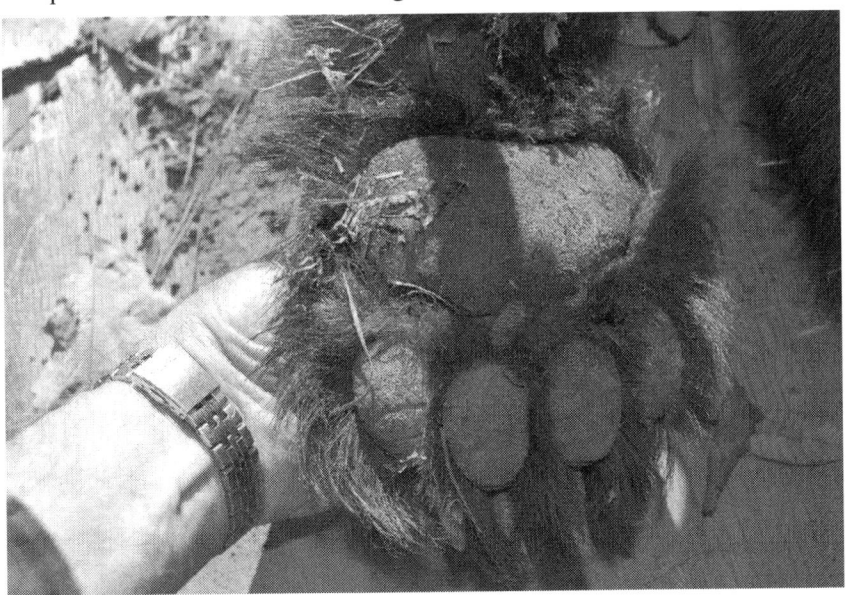

Bears have huge paws!

Apparently, this young female liked the city life in Atlanta, because that's where she was captured again as a nuisance bear.

"When bears are really, really disturbed, it seems like from what I've read and seen that sometimes they will make these huge movements, and they just keep going," said Kacy. "Even though you drop them off in good habitat, they sometimes just keep moving. That's what this bear did. From Atlanta, she was transported to Oaky Woods and tranquilized."

Although this bear wasn't a Middle Georgia bear, WRD decided to equip her with a radio collar anyway. After all, maybe she'd find the swamps of Middle Georgia home and she'd one day provide some accountable information. This wasn't the case.

"She had a lip tattoo — she was No. 19 in another study," said Kacy. "Scott McDonald (WRD biologist) called all these people trying to find out where she'd come from, and that's how we found out she originally came from Gatlinburg. They let her go behind the house I lived in at Oaky Woods (WMA). The next day she was four miles south and I just knew she was going to keep going."

South of the WMA there is a lot of agricultural land, and Kacy said bears prefer areas with cover. The next night Kacy followed the bear the entire night with radio-tracking equipment.

"She crossed the Ocmulgee River first thing the next morning in a span of 15 minutes," said Kacy. "The males in the study have crossed the river, but none of the females have. She turned northeast and kept going. She moved four miles a day and she kept moving on that same compass bearing. I could go back home, look at a map and predict where she'd be the next day. I'd drive an hour from my house, and sure enough I'd pick up her signal. I followed her for the next week."

While Kacy and another student were tracking the female bear they noticed that she was showing a preference to forested areas, avoiding fields when possible. While tracking very early one morning, they were listening to the signal from a highway. The bear was moving through an expansive block of woods, heading right for their location. The big woods the bear was cruising in was quickly narrowing down into a bottleneck with fields on both sides.

"We just knew she was going to come right down that line of woods, and sure enough she crossed right in front of us," said Kacy. "We watched her run across — it was neat. Black bears are super smart at navigation."

Kacy said that Lynn Rogers, one of the world's more famous bear researchers, has experience with bear memory and bear navigation. He claims bears have better navigational skill than humans and an incredible memory of places.

"One of the things bears will do is take these very extensive excursions, and for males in our study we've seen them move up to 20 miles — the longest female was a little more than five miles (other than the one just mentioned)," said Kacy. "These bears will go to a new area, explore it for a while, then go back to first area."

It may not sound that amazing on paper, but try walking 20 miles in the woods, spend a few days stumbling around and then turn around and go right back where you can from. These return trips back into familiar territory have been common with the bears in the study, but the traveling nuisance bear probably won't be back to visit the bottomland hardwoods of Oaky Woods WMA. That bear ended up crossing I-16 very quickly one morning, and Kacy never got another reading on her.

"There is a lot more forest north of I-16, and I think she had more (travel areas) to choose from," said Kacy.

Reports of a collared bear started coming into DNR around the Bartow, Wadley and Thomson areas in McDuffie County. A few days later a fisherman on Clarks Hill Lake near Lincolnton reported a bear wearing a radio collar swimming across the lake into South Carolina. Although it's not confirmed that this is the Oaky Woods bear, chances are good.

When bears are really distressed there is the potential for them to make big movements," said Kacy. "No studies have been able to document a large emigration where they believed a bear was being monitored and all of a sudden it just left."

Kacy said there was a study in Florida, where a distressed bear left Eglin Air Force Base and was found in Baton Rouge, Louisiana. Who knows were the Oaky Woods bear was heading when it swam across Clarks Hill.

"She knew what she was doing when she got across I-16 real fast," said Kacy. "Some bears know how to cross roads, especially if they've been hit and survive. Potentially, she already knew how to cross roads because she did get through Atlanta."

Kacy said she believes one of the bears in the WRD study was hit during the summer by a vehicle on Hwy 96, the main road along the north side of Ocmulgee WMA.

"One of the bears that received a collar would cross the road near the river on Hwy 96 day after day," said Kacy. "One morning the DNR received a call that a bear had been hit near the railroad tracks early in the morning. They couldn't find the bear lying next to the road. Later that day we were driving down the road and this male's collar signal came in super loud. I got a reading on him, and he was only 100 meters from the highway. I called DNR and asked where the bear was hit, and they said by the railroad tracks. That was where the bear's signal was so strong. They came back out and were going to walk in on him but didn't because they were concerned about safety issues. If he was injured he could have gone at them.

Over the next week Kacy kept a close watch on the bear using only her telemetry equipment to see if the bear had moved. For a solid week, the bear just sat in one spot, a behavior that no other bear in the study would do, at least in the summer months. Below, a bear sniffs a sardine can.

"We thought he was going to die of starvation and dehydration," said Kacy. "Then he got up and started moving again. He crossed the highway a couple of more times after that, and he just headed south. We don't know if it's true, but I feel like he was the bear hit by the car and he was spending his time recovering."

The fact that the bear left the area around the busy highway because it was hit by a car is pure speculation, but it does make you wonder if he was smarter than the average bear.

Although WRD's bear study is far from over, Kacy has spent enough time with radio-telemetry equipment in her hands to learn a few things about these bears home-range sizes and denning behavior.

Kacy said bears shift their home ranges seasonally. Mid to late summer is when some of the bears will begin to explore new areas for a few weeks, but they'll return to where they came from. Three out of 12 males went 20 miles, and other males went as little as four miles before their return. Female bears also shifted their home range at this time, only on a smaller scale. The longest female excursion, not counting the Gatlinburg bear, was just 5 1/2 miles. An average female excursion was 2 1/2 miles.

"When the bears made their return, they'd stay there for a few weeks and then shift their home range back to the area they explored," said Kacy. "This area ended up being the bear's fall and winter area, and they'd stay there throughout the winter."

It has been documented that while in their winter haunts some bears will den for a period of time.

"When you talk about hibernating in the south, a bear's metabolism does lower and their body temperatures lower somewhat, but it's not near to the extent that bears hibernate in the north," said Kacy. "Some of the females began denning in early January, and two of the females denned until the end of April. They stayed at one den the whole time."

In the south, Kacy said other studies have shown that black bears will generally have multiple dens and make movements during warmer periods. She hasn't correlated her winter movement data with temperatures yet.

"Two females with cubs in 2003 didn't den at all," said Kacy. "One was constantly moving between resting areas, where she'd have locations inside a 500-square-meter area.

"Another female who had cubs appeared to den for one month from the end of January to end of February. After that she'd make these small localized movements into early April until the movements gradually would get larger, but they'd center on the den. I don't know what's going on there, but it's interesting." (4)

The males generally moved toward areas of agricultural fields by November looking for high-protein food, and they'd stay through the winter. Kacy said those bears would move very little, staying around the food.

By spring the bears in the study generally were headed back to their summer home ranges. Some of males in the study moved to hunting clubs to feed on deer feed and winter wheat.

"One day I got a close signal on this one male, so I wanted to make sure he was there. I drove into the field, and there he was," said Kacy. "The next day I found an older, heavier male in the same field, and that younger male was two kilometers away. It's believed that the subdominant males are pushed out of feeding areas by dominant males." (To cite a couple of other examples, Bobby Bond said one male bear regularly travels between Tarversville in Twiggs County to Clinchfield in Houston County, about 12 miles away. Another male that was captured and collared in the Oaky Woods Wildlife Management Area in Houston is now a resident of Telfair County, about 50 miles away.)

Using the current bear data that WRD now has, home-range size for a female varied from 5.5 to 18 miles and averaged 15 square miles. The males home range is much larger — varying between 24 and 468 square miles and averaging 173 square miles. Black bears have populated middle Georgia for thousands of years and hopefully with proper management they'll continue to strive here. Young male bears like to seek out new territory in the spring, so hopefully the population will continue to expand.

Because of concern about the high kill rate on female bears, the Georgia DNR did take positive action in 2017 to move the middle Georgia bear hunt into January, when more female bears would be denning, and less likely to be harvested by hunters. On the January 13, 2018 bear hunt, two bears were taken, one male and one female. It was a cold and windy day which lowered the harvest, and the harvest can be expected to fluctuate from year to year.

According to Kevin Kramer, Region Supervisor for the Fort Valley DNR office, The DNR is still working on a "Population Viability Assessment" with researcher Mike Hooker that will try to determine the overall health status of the middle Georgia bear population. By continuing to seek good information, I'm confident that the Georgia DNR will make the right call in managing this small bear population. Hopefully, with careful management this middle Georgia population will continue to thrive and survive long into the future.

The map below shows the concentration s of bears in Oaky Woods and Ocmulgee WMA'S in Houston and Twiggs Counties. A few will wander into surrounding counties.

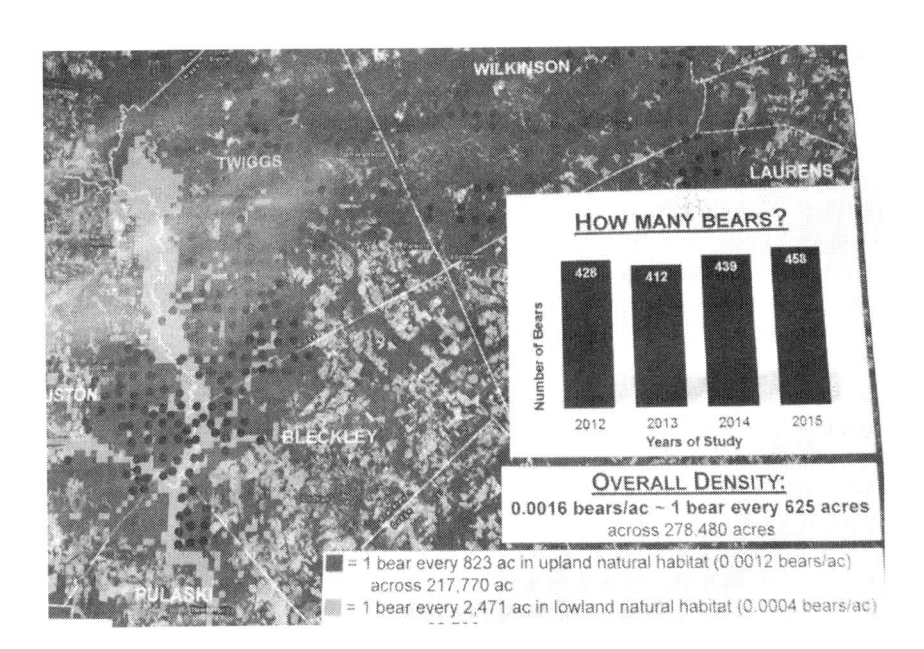

1)"Bear Population Lower that thought", Macon Telegraph, Wayne Crenshaw

2) 'One Day Hunt kills 10% of Mid-state Bears" Macon Telegraph, Heather Duncan, December 27 ,2011

3) "More bears than though in Middle Georgia?' Macon Telegraph, Wayne Crenshaw, December 12, 2016

4)"Tales from Middle Georgia Bear Woods"- Brad Gill, 2012 Georgia Outdoor News

CHAPTER 6

TWO BEARS TAKEN IN MIDDLE GA HUNT ON JANUARY 13, 2018

Jeff Mitchell had taken lots of game animals over the years, but when a black bear stepped out into the food plot at 6:05 pm, it was something very special. He said he felt a quickened pulse and a nervousness in his fingers that he had not felt for several years of hunting and hoped the opportunity did not slip away. But the unsuspecting bear eased through the food plot and gave Jeff the chance to center his scope on the bear's chest. When he sent the 270 Winchester slug on its way, the bear quickly dropped, but popped back up, trying to escape. But a second anchoring shot finished the story. Jeff had his first ever bear and he was excited!

After a round of photos, the bear was taken down to the Oaky Woods Check station so that Georgia DNR staff could gather important biological information. The bear was a 140-pound female and was taken in Twiggs County on the Bear Creek hunting club. The majority of the bears taken on the central Georgia Bear hunt have come from Twiggs County, with a few from Houston County and only one from Bibb County since the hunts started in 2011. Jeff is from Atlanta and owns his own Company, Mitchell Metals, where he specializes in custom awnings and coverings for schools and businesses.

The one-day Middle Georgia Bear hunt was held on January 13, 2018, and two bears were killed by lucky hunters. The hunt is held on private properties in Twiggs, Houston and Bibb Counties and is limited to one bear over one hundred pounds and bears with cubs are protected. No bear hunting is allowed on Oaky Woods or Ocmulgee WMA'S; thus, these areas act as a refuge for the bears.

The other bear was taken by Jay Bonney in Twiggs County, in the western part of the county on private land near Adams Park Road. Jay got invited to hunt on a lease and was expecting a wild pig to show itself but was aware of the chance for a bear and was ready for the opportunity. He had only been on the stand for 30 minutes when the bear eased into the small green food plot. The bear looked big enough and he slowly pulled the trigger of his 30-06 and sent the 150 grain Remington

Core-Lokt bullet on its mission. The bear quickly dropped, and Jay had harvested his first bear and he was one very happy hunter! The bear was processed and taken to a local Taxidermist, so it could be converted into a rug, then the great memories could be relived for many years. Jay works at Mercer University in Macon where he deals with Student IDs and security systems.

Jay and Jeff are a growing group of Georgia hunters who have been successful in pursuing home- grown Georgia bears. The north Georgia bear population is robust with a limit of two bears, while the bear population in south -Georgia, near the Okefenokee Swamp, is stable with a limit of one bear. The middle Georgia bear hunt is held with the states smallest population, with a limit of one bear, and is estimated around 458 bears over 217,770 acres in central Georgia. The middle Georgia population estimate has varied in recent years, with early estimates around 300 bears. In 2015, after three years of study, Georgia's Warnell School of forestry estimated that the population was only 140 bears. But researchers later re- analyzed the same data, using different mathematical models and estimated 240 bears a brief time later. The latest estimate, using a more liberal statistical model and a larger geographical area, estimated 458 bears, according to Annaliese Ashley, UGA Grad student. But the population may be down a bit from previous years, according to Area Regional Biologist Supervisor Kevin Kramer, who says that bear nuisance complains are down, which usually indicates less bears roaming around into human populated areas.

Mike Hooker, University of Georgia Bear Researcher, say he is still working on a central Georgia bear viability study which looks a wide variety of bear population dynamics which will be used to manage this small population in the future. The central Georgia bear hunt started in its present form in 2011 when 34 bears were killed on a mid- November hunt. Due to concerns about baiting and the high harvest of female bears, the hunt was moved to December. The high harvest of sow bears was a concern as they are the driving force of the population, especially in a small population, as bears don't normally breed until they are three years old and a sow will stay with her cubs for two years, according to Kramer. Although this year's harvest was low at two bears, fifty percent of the harvest was female, which the DNR will consider in future regulation planning. There are other losses to the population, which must be considered and in 2017, a total of 17 bears were reported as road kill and one was mistaken for a wild pig, which is a significant yearly loss, according to Bobby Bond, Region Game Biologist.

For 2018, the Georgia DNR moved the hunt to January so that more sow bears might be denning, but the hunt is highly dependent on the weather, says Kramer. This hunt was held on a cold, windy day which probably limited bear activity in the morning, but some bears were moving in the afternoon, when both bears were taken. With all the acorns gone late in the season, hunting green food plots, which the bears will eat in a crunch with limited food sources, is a good hunting strategy, as both hunters proved this year. The next hunt is scheduled for Saturday, January 12, 2019, and the middle Georgia Bear hunt is a unique opportunity to harvest a special game animal, so start making plans!

Jeff Mitchell harvested this nice Black Bear in Twiggs County on the Jan 13 hunt

CHAPTER 7
CLYDE YODER'S TIPS FOR OAKY WOODS BUCKS

Clyde Yoder's friends jokingly tell him that he's such a lucky hunter that he could put up a stand on the light pole at the Wal-Mart parking lot and probably shoot a buck. But Yoder, a very modest and humble hunter, says he welcomes good luck and it always helps to be at the right place at the right time. However, he says it is more important to do your homework and be properly prepared, and then when your chance comes, you can make the shot! Yoder has an uncanny ability to "make the shot" and in recent years has put an impressive number of good bucks on the ground, and those bucks did not come from some privately-owned lease, but from Georgia WMA'S!

Yoder first came to this writer's attention in 2011 when he brought a very nice buck into the check station at Oaky Woods WMA during the early December deer hunt. The wide racked 10 pointer was one of the best bucks taken last year from Oaky Woods, but I happened to remember that he brought in another good buck in 2010, and that I had also seen him in previous years, usually at the check station with game in the rear of his truck. This kind of continued success has a way of getting your attention, so recently I sat down with Yoder to pick his brain about his hunting techniques and he was generous in sharing information that might help other hunters.

Clyde Yoder, of Montezuma, displays a few of his nicer bucks taken from Oaky Woods, Ocmulgee, Piedmont Refuge and other Public hunting locations.

We met at his small office at the Mid-Georgia Farm Supply store, just outside Montezuma, Georgia, in the heart of the Mennonite farming community. Yoder is owner- operator of his own company and his principal job is spreading fertilizer and lime in the thousands of acres under cultivation in central Georgia and the farms here are among the best managed in the state. Yoder's family was originally from the Virginia Beach area and they were among the first Mennonites to settle in central Georgia. Today, the Mennonites operate a very successful farming operation in Macon County and are a very important part of the Macon County business and civic community. Yoder has moved around a bit, but he has been a dedicated hunter of state WMA'S since 1990, a relatively short time to experience such good success.

Most hunters know that Macon County is either at the top, or near the top of GON's best locations to kill a good buck in Georgia every year, which begs the question, why would a Macon County resident with many local contacts, hunt on public land? To Yoder, the answer to that question is simple and it's a matter of economics. He explained that many years ago it was common for landowners to let friends hunt on their land without charge. However, with landowners trying to stretch every dollar, the good money brought in by leasing land to hunters was too much to ignore, and cheap lease land dried up. That prompted Yoder to check out other alternatives. He couldn't help but notice that for the cost of a hunting license and $19.00 for a WMA stamp he could hunt on thousands of acres across the state on the many wildlife management areas. But Yoder has decreased his cost of hunting even further by purchasing lifetime hunting and fishing license. Instead of shelling out $62.00 every year for a sportsman's license, he bought the lifetime license for $500 and only after a few years he was hunting for free! He says more hunters would do the math, they would buy the lifetime license. For example, a lifetime license for a child under two is only $200, so parents and grandparents, take notice!

Oaky Woods Manager, Raye Jones, left and Ken Grahl, right, Region Biologist, both now retired, congratulate a hunter on his nice buck

Although he was somewhat apprehensive about hunting on public land, the low cost and easy accessibility was very tempting, so he gave it a try and has been pleased with his results. One of the important things about hunting public land, says Yoder, is the ease of the hunting experience. When hunting leased land, Yoder says there was always the problem of getting other hunters to share the cost of the lease, the expense of maintaining the food plots and keeping up the roads. Then every year there was the scheduled work days to maintain the camp and deer stands. But WMA hunting is relatively simple, just follow the rules, check in or sign in for the hunt and go hunting! With much more land to hunt, Yoder says he no longer must hunt the same few stands every year on a small lease and the ability to scout new locations every year on different WMA's and this makes the hunting experience more enjoyable for him. Of course, there are a few negatives, like limited hunting days on most WMA's and having to share the land with other hunters, but Yoder's says these are minor inconveniences. To cope with limited hunting days, he carefully plans his hunt dates, then moves around to various WMA's that are open. To cope with other hunters, he says that a little common courtesy to others goes a long way.

Tommy Shover, Oaky Woods Manager, is doing a wonderful job and posts some photos of nice bucks taken on a recent hunt on the Check station wall. Everyone wants to know if big bucks are falling!

Although Yoder hunts many WMA's, his favorites tend to be a

short drive from his home and he does the bulk of his hunting on Oaky Woods, Cedar creek, Ocmulgee and Rum Creek WMA's and he also hunts Piedmont National Refuge every year. One of his WMA hunting techniques is to pick a spot where you can see as far as possible. This sounds simple but is effective. His best buck to date is a 13 pointer with a 16 inch inside spread from Cedar Creek WMA, taken in 2005. Yoder and a large number of his friends go the Cedar Creek hunts each year and camp out and they always bring out a lot of deer. Yoder was hunting one of his usual spots where he could see 50 -75 yards around a creek bottom and a trail that crossed the creek showed many fresh deer tracks. But because the upper tree canopy was thick, he left the climber stand in the truck and just hunted from a folding chair, a low tech but effective way to hunt sometimes, says Yoder. He was in his stand 45 minutes before first light and soon after the sun lit up the woods a fat doe ambled by and she stopped to look over her shoulder. Thinking that the doe might have company, he waited a few minutes and soon the 13-pointer came by with his nose high in the air, trailing the doe. A single shot from his Marlin Bolt action rifle in 270-caliber put the buck on the ground. But he wasn't finished yet! The woods were still echoing from his rifle blast when a nice five pointer ran by and he put it down also, thus his Cedar Creek hunt was over with plenty of venison to show for the effort. Yoder is a meat hunter, but the bucks have tended to show up in his sites frequently and last year he bagged five bucks on Georgia WMA's, one buck in Alabama and two does and all the meat went in his freezer. He only had to fill in his deer tag information for one deer as all the WMA deer receive a special WMA tag that does not count against a hunter yearly limit of 12 deer, another bonus of WMA hunting, says Yoder. Below,

Clyde Yoder with nice Cedar Creek WMA Buck

He says he hunts for concentrations of deer, and, "if you find the does, you will find the bucks". That is why he doesn't concern himself too much with rubs and scrape line, but instead concentrates on bottlenecks where deer cross creeks, transition areas where pines open into hardwoods or openings where he can see a long distance. Last year on Oaky Woods WMA, he found a creek crossing with thick cover on both sides that forced the deer into a bottle neck and set up his climbing stand. Early the next morning a doe ambled by and he shot it, killing it instantly. After the woods quieted, he decided to set a little longer and see what else he might see and within a few minutes the nice buck came walking by and Yoder nailed it too, so his hunt was over! The chore of getting the deer back to the truck was made easier with his two-wheel pull cart that he also carries with him.

A big part of Yoder hunting strategy on WMA's is "other hunter control'. He says many hunters stumble into the woods at daybreak and they spook deer in the process. That's why he is on the stand well before first light so that a confused deer is more likely to come by. Also, he does not rely on cover scents or scent control clothes to hide his scent, he just gets higher in his stand, usually 20 plus feet if conditions permit, so deer normally miss his scent. To further use other hunter's movements to his advantage, he often hunts on stand all day, while most other hunters head to the truck for lunch. He has often taken deer from 11 am to 2pm for this reason. Also, while a lot of hunters start heading to the truck as the sun starts to set, he frequently stays on his stand until dark and comes out with a flash light, waiting to the last minute to hopefully see a deer moved by other hunters. But sometimes Yoder tries a different approach to hunting WMA's. Sometimes he would like to get away from other hunters. He tries to find the most remote hunting locations on the WMA. He is hunting and usually these are spots more than a half mile from the nearest road, which is further than most hunters want to walk to hunt. Then the thinking is to hunt undisturbed deer which also pays off as deer will be following their natural movement patterns. So, whether it's hunter control on crowded hunts or hunting remote locations, Yoder says they both work!

One last thing that Yoder does to stay both physically and mentally fit for hunting is to hunt all year. If the deer season is over, he will most likely be in some farmer's field tracking down wild pigs and he shoots lots of pigs each year that are damaging crops. Come deer season you will probably see him at a middle Georgia WMA check station with game in the back of his truck!

CHAPTER 8

HUNT FROM THE GROUND IN OAKY WOODS

As a young boy I remember climbing trees to explore the world around me. Things always looked pretty special from 10 to 15 feet off the ground. Then after many tree-climbing episodes the inevitable happened! I was about 10 feet off the ground and as I was climbing an oak tree my foot slipped, and I did not have a tight enough hand grip. Before I could say "Oops", I was falling to the ground. I don't remember the fall too much, but I sure remember the stop when I hit the ground!

I knew I was still alive because I was in terrible pain! My lungs were on fire because I held my breath on the fall and when I hit the ground, all the air in my lungs rushed from my chest, like a popping balloon. My daddy would tell me later that I got the breath knocked out of me. Lying on the ground, looking at the sky, I wondered why I could not breathe or even cry out in pain. I could hardly moan! It took several minutes, but slowly I regained my breath and composure. Shortly thereafter, I found myself somewhat better educated through the "hard knocks of life" and quit climbing trees for recreation.

John Trussell was a poor college student back in 1972 when he shot this nice 10 pointer from a ground blind in Oaky Woods.

However, in the late 1960's we all started to deer hunt and those with advanced brains told us it was time to start climbing trees, so we could get our human scent above the noses of the deer and remain undetected in the woods. So back into the trees I went, this time by way of a climbing tree stand. I climbed hundreds of trees and shot lots of deer, then the inevitable happened again. I was high up a tree in a climbing stand on a cold, wet day, when I decided to come down. In trying to loosen the stand from the tree, I turned toward the tree. I put my feet close to the tree and then the "V' notch of the stand lost its grip on the bark before I had a good grip on the hand bar and was ready to descend. In a brief dash of terror, I was rushing to the ground in a near free fall! I tried to hold onto the tree to no avail, but my thick coat at least kept most of the skin on my arms. I crashed into the ground and was able to extract myself from the foot hold straps on the stand with only a few bruises. I was very lucky that I had not fallen over backward and broke my legs as has happened to other hunters.

On another occasion, many years ago, I was helping with a hunting club work day and we were doing yearly maintenance on club deer stands. They had stands built into trees, this was a really bad idea, and as I climbed the wooden steps, one step about 6 feet off the ground broke. Before I could say, 'Oops", I was falling down the side of the tree. The bottom step was a large nail, another bad idea, and my rear end caught the nail as I was falling. The nail put a round cut on my wallet, which literally saved my butt! Hunting from the ground started looking a whole lot better! Lessons learned- don't ever drive nails into trees and don't hunt or even work or repair old wood stands build in trees!

John Trussell was stalking through the woods when he shot this wild boar with a 22 magnum.

My accidents happened before hunter safety got serious press, but now after years of accidents and tree stand deaths, modern technology has made climbing trees much safer. However, hunters are still much more at risk from falling from a tree that they are from being injured or killed by firearms accidents. I don't climb many trees to deer hunt any more, but when I do, I use the Hunter Safety System (**www.huntersafetysystem.com** or 256-773-7732) which involves using a chest vest/harness paired with a tree strap and sliding safety rope that allows hunters to safely climb, sit in a tree stand and descend a tree without danger. I highly recommend that hunters use this system.

I have been hunting from the ground for many years and let the terrain, the amount of leaves on trees and the distance I must travel to drag a deer out of the woods as primary factors that help me decide the best strategy for any hunt. When I hunt at Piedmont Refuge, for example, I usually walk a long distance from the road to get away from other hunters and almost always just take in a lightweight folding dove stool. Last year I found a line of scrapes about three quarters of a mile from my truck and put the dove stool just below the ridge line and leaned up against a big tree to hide my outline. I also made sure I was downwind from the location where I expected the deer to appear.

I got into location before daylight and about an hour later I noticed a big buck easing along, more interested in finding a doe than eating. Moving my rifle into position only when the buck was looking the other way, I finally got on target and dropped the 13-point buck into the leaves with my 270 Winchester 270, loaded with 130 grain Hornady light magnum bullets. That long trip back to my truck was helped by the fact that I did not also have to carry a 50-pound tree climbing stand!

Another alternative to a climbing deer stand is a four-legged quad condo stand, or tree house stand. Built of aluminum or heavy pipe for legs and a plastic shelter on top, these are becoming more popular, but can be pricey. You still must use a ladder to access the blind, but if build properly and maintained, they are safe when using due caution. Many hunters build their own from 4x4 posts and leg kits which reduces the cost. If you have a long-term lease or own your own land, these are worth considering. For more information on these, check out wwwbuckhornwr.com or 800-442-4147. But now back to ground blind hunting. This simple hunting method is very safe and effective, and more hunters should try it! Here are some of the techniques and advantages of hunting from the ground.

A big benefit of hunting from the ground is safety. Sitting on a ground stool is about as safe as it gets, and if you fall asleep and tumble to the ground it won't normally hurt you. P.S- don't try sleeping in stands 15 feet off the ground!

Ground stools and ground camo blinds are very simple to use and light weight to carry. Many brands of camo ground blinds use flat steel coil springs that when released, basically set up the blind for you. Take down is simple too, but some of the larger blinds require a little more work.

Ground blinds protect you from the wind and rain and if you hunt with young hunters with you, they can move around a little bit without spooking the deer. Human scent is somewhat contained within the blind if you keep the windows openings to a minimum and a good cover scent helps too.

Visibility from a ground blind can be outstanding as it is below the limb line and the situation improves as the leaves start hitting the ground in the fall. Visibility from a tree stand is often limited to the area beneath the tree unless a lot of limb trimming is done. To make your ground blind quieter, rake out he leaves beneath your feet and smear a little chap stick on the zippers to keep them quiet. To make it harder for the deer to spot you in the blind, set in the middle and not next to a window and use a face mask. When possible, set up your ground blind a few days ahead of using it so the deer are used to seeing it in the landscape. After you have harvested several deer from your ground blind, you mind wonder why you don't hunt this way more often! Good luck in the deer woods this fall!

CHAPTER 9
BIG BUCKS COME INTO OAKY WOODS AND OCMULGEE WMA'S CHECK STATIONS

(This story by author, Georgia Outdoor News- December 2008)

Don Edwards could not believe his eyes. He had just looked down from his deer stand, latched onto a tree in area six of the Ocmulgee WMA, located in Bleckley, Pulaski and Twiggs Counties. He saw a spike buck and let it go by, hoping it might wander by his son who was further down the trail. But a couple of seconds later he looked back over his shoulder and saw this huge buck standing in front of his stand. Trying not to concentrate on the large rack, he fired his 30-06 rifle and the monster buck went down quickly. At 10:00 am, he climbed down from his stand, lifted the head of the huge buck and realized that he had just harvested the biggest buck of his life!

With 20 points and a sixteen and four -eights outside spread, the buck dressed out at 152 pounds. Back at the Ocmulgee check station, Biologist Bobby Bond and WMA Manager Randy Wood determined that the buck was six and a half years old, which is the oldest buck to ever come off the WMA. The buck is a strong contender to be the best buck from a WMA during the 2008-09 season, but the clock is still running. Edwards is a Sargent with the Warner Robins Police Department and has hunted Ocmulgee WMA for many years. Another nice 12-point buck was killed on the Thanksgiving Ocmulgee hunt by David Cox of Warner Robins. Cox was hunting in some planted pines near Albert Jenkins Road, when he saw a doe pop out of the woods, followed by the buck at about 9:40 am and he shot it with a 243 rifle. He was rewarded for his patience because it was raining, and he had briefly gotten out of his stand to install an umbrella over his stand so he could continue hunting. He had previously experienced a slow year deer hunting and had only seen three deer all season, but he sure cashed in his chips with this great buck!

According to DNR Biologist Bobby Bond, Ocmulgee WMA had 733 hunters check in for the November 26-29 hunt and they killed 121 deer, 28 does and 93 bucks for a success ratio of 16.5 percent. Earlier, on the Nov 1-7 hunt, 397 hunters killed 21 bucks for a success ratio of five percent.

Over on Oaky Woods WMA in Houston and Pulaski Counties, the early December hunt is popular because it coincides with the end of the rut and some big bucks show up at the check station and this hunt proved to be a good one!

David Karwacki, left, and Josh Kirkland, both from the Georgia coast, both shot big bucks and may be the first hunters to bring high tech hunting to Oaky Woods through text messaging!

On Wednesday, December 3, Josh texted David, who was hunting in another area, "Hey, shot a big one! David responded, "Need any help?" Josh texted-"Nope, it is prime time, stay in your stand". A few minute later, David texted " Hey, I shot a big one too! Meet you at the check station!" Hunting on Oaky Woods will never be the same! These two guys are regular hunters at Oaky Woods WMA and Karwacki said that Oaky Woods may be the best non-quota big buck hunt in the state of Georgia and he tries to hunt it every year. Karwacki's buck was 3.5 years old, weighted 168 live and had a 19 and three-eighths inch outside spread, while Kirkland's buck was a 5.5-year-old, weighted 185 live and had a seventeen and five-eighths spread.

Although success often favors the hunter who is well experienced in hunting an area, Eddie Dunn of Lizella proved that micro scouting a small area can pay off too! On his first Oaky Woods hunt,

Dunn saw some tall oak trees not far from the check station that over looked a clear cut that had a small deer trail running through it. It was only about 200 yards off the most traveled road in the WMA and Dunn could clearly see hundreds of vehicles passing by from his elevated perch and they could see him, but the deer did not seem to mind the noise. Late in the morning, he saw a doe amble by and it was followed by huge eight pointer that he stretched out with a good shot.

Alan Davis of Loganville checked in a great tall tined buck after he ambushed it in a funnel area. It was a 3.5-year-old eight pointer with a 17-inch spread and was taken in area five. Other notable bucks were: D.C Maddox of commerce hunts with a group of 15 from his area every year and he killed a good eight pointer. Dennis Plank of Montezuma shot two nice bucks, a 10 pointer and an eight pointer, 30 minutes apart! More good bucks were taken by John Lang, WT Clark, Brant Carey, William Clack, James Sumner, Marlon Eldridge, Victor Williams, James Lamarca and Tommy Hensley. Claude Coile of Acworth did it the hard way and collected a good doe with his 300-whisper caliber, Thompson Contender pistol.

According to Oaky Woods Manager Raye Jones and Biologist Bobby Bond, 521 hunters checked in for the Dec 3-6 buck - doe hunt and 111 deer were killed, 35 does and 76 bucks. This equates to a 21 percent success ratio which is excellent for a late season WMA hunt. Not counted in the success ratio is the wild hog harvest and about 20 hogs were brought by the check station. On an earlier hunt, on Nov 8-14, 418 hunters shot 38 bucks for a success ratio of nine percent.

The author at the old school bus body that is a major landmark on the Oaky Woods map and sits on an old homestead site. It is from a mid-1960's hunting camp.

These two WMA's are the heart of middle Georgia hunting and their futures are cloudy. On the good side, Ocmulgee is 50 percent state owned, with a large tract around the check station being purchased a few years ago. But a large 4,000 tract, north of highway 96, may be doubtful for the future, but it's status varies from year to year, according to Kevin Kramer, DNR Region Game Management Supervisor. Just a few years ago, Ocmulgee WMA consisted of 29,000 acres, now it is 21,243 and the state has no secure funding source to purchase valuable and disappearing conservation properties.

Don Edwards dropped this nice buck in Ocmulgee WMA across from Oaky Woods

Oaky Woods is in the most endangered as it is owned by an investment group interested in putting a huge residential and commercial community on the property. However, for the present time the state can continue to lease the property, but on a year to year basis, which is true for all WMA leases. Charles Ayer, the principle manager of the Oaky Woods Property and the owner of the Sports Center in Perry, recently told this writer that he supports public hunting on WMA'S and he and his co-owners have agreed not to ask for a lease increase in the upcoming year because he knows the state is in a financial crunch. His said his property tax and insurance is 11.25 per acre and the state pays 12.50 per acre for the property, so the owners are only at the break- even point. He said he has closely monitored the community discussion in Houston County about the importance of Oaky Woods and is open minded about any proposals that might purchase and preserve Oaky Woods as a WMA. The Houston County Commissioners have recently stated that they would be in favor of letting citizens vote on a small bond issue that would combine with state and private funds to purchase Oaky Woods, but all state funds have dried up because of the recession, thus future discussions are on hold. But will the state have the funds to continue leasing Oaky Woods in the short term?

John Bowers, the DNR Ass.t Chief of Game Management, said nothing is firm with the budget process and they are closely monitoring, with OPB, the state's financial condition, but right now WMA leases on private property are not on the table for cuts, but that doesn't mean they won't be in the future. Present discussions are on removing state services from National forest lands, but those lands will remain open for public hunting. Bowers said the DNR has made the Governor's office aware of the departments concerns about the possible loss of WMA's and he says Oaky Woods has High Quality habitat near high population centers and gets a lot of use. In addition, Oaky Woods is home to the isolated middle Georgia black bear population that only numbers about 300 bears, according to a recent DNR study and Bowers said Oaky Woods provides vital bear habitat. These factors are important considerations when the DNR weighs the important of each WMA. Hopefully, the future of Ocmulgee and Oaky Woods WMA's will be stable in the future and outdoorsmen can continue to enjoy the excellent hunting there. As the deer season winds down, don't forget that both areas have good small game hunting, including wild pigs, so come on down!

CHAPTER 10
CLEAR CUT: WHERE'S THE DEER?

The words *clear cut* strike uneasiness among hunters who lease land, or potential hunter's owners who are looking to buy land for its hunting potential. It can also spell changes for hunters on WMA'S like Oaky Woods. A few years ago, some friends and I were in a hunting club and we got word from the owner that the property would be clear cut during the summer. Our question was what impact would the clear cut have on our hunting the next fall? Would the deer leave the area?

Posted on the check station wall- David Blan, nice 10 pointer

We feared the worst and knew that the hardwood ridges and bottoms we loved to hunt would soon be gone and replanted in pines. Was it time to let the lease lapse and look for new property or should we hold on to the property?

These questions are *"what ifs"* but more and more lease holders and potential property owners face these questions on a frequent basis. This article will try to provide some answers. The first fact we must confront is that forests are dynamic, ever changing pieces of property. It's been said that *"the only constant in life is change."* This applies to forests very appropriately since they are probably this country's most valuable renewable resource.

Trees grow, then are harvested and replanted. It's a situation that as hunters we don't always like, but we cope around it best we can. There are not many landowners who can let land set idle without producing income in the form of a lease, timber production or both.

As hunters, however, we must decide what impact clear cutting or in some cases, select cutting, has on game populations, especially deer and turkey. To answer these questions, I spoke with Dr. Robert L. "Larry" Marchinton, Professor of Wildlife Biology at the University of Georgia and well -known supporter of quality deer management. Our first question was *"When an area is clear cut, what happens to the deer?"*

"Naturally the deer move off due to the human activity and lack of cover, but I don't think they move off as far as you might think," says Marchinton.

"Deer move off to adjacent properties but in many cases grasses and browse emerge again within a few months and the deer start moving back in to some extent. Excellent browse in the form of honeysuckle, greenbrier, blackberry, and other palatable vegetation draw in the deer. It should be remembered that although most producing trees like water oaks and red oaks produce all their deer food in the early fall when the acorns hit the ground; but within a few months most of the acorns are gone. So, while the acorns impact is very positive and an important food source in the fall to help build up the deer reserves for the winter, diversity in food sources and habitats are important too. "

"Clear-cuts help to provide that needed diversity and provide good nutritional browse in the spring and summer. So, while it's true that clear cutting has a temporary negative impact on the deer, the land soon recovers, and the deer soon return."

Are there any other benefits of clear cutting to deer?

"Yes, besides the browse food, clear cuts provide thick cover that helps to protect the age structure of bucks and ensures that some will survive to quality buck dimensions. sometimes it's not pleasant to hunt in a thick area but the deer will readily move into the thick bushes to hide and it also provides a good bedding area.

"Especially in the piedmont area where the mature forests are fairly open, it's important to have clear cuts that emerge again because they provide that browse and thick refuge the bucks needs, and these characteristics are hard to provide with any other type of habitat.

"Next to my property near Athens we have a former clear cut that is now growing with 6 - 7 year- old pines and thick brush. Besides the benefits to the deer I'm seeing bobcats and other wildlife that I did not see before the thick brush was available."

How is the hunting on clear cuts?

Marchinton says that the first year or two after cutting, the hunting results on open land may be disappointing, but hunting around the fringes and along creeks and bottom lands which act as travel corridors for the deer can be very productive. Food plots interspersed around the property can also draw in deer from surrounding properties until the clear-cut browse becomes re-established. Tall ladder stands, and tower stands can be highly successful on clear cut because of the long ranges that can be covered. Marchinton advises hunters to carefully scrutinize the terrain of a clear cut because deer can get sneaky.

He once saw a buck crawling on its knees through a clear cut and feels that this behavior, while unusual, is not all that uncommon. Once the brush and browse on a clear cut gets up more than 3 - 4 feet, the tall deer stands in place may diminish in effectiveness, naturally. But hunters can try to locate ground blinds near well- worn trails or establish *"firing lanes"* through the brush to get a clear shot at any deer that might pass through.

As far as deer hunting is concerned, is it better to "select cut" certain sizes of timber as opposed to clear cutting?

Marchinton says it is difficult to answer this question because there are as many types of select cutting as there are property owners. However, in general terms, select cutting means selecting certain varieties of trees in specific sizes to be harvested. For example, one owner might choose to cut all hardwoods and pines over 6 inches in diameter.

While select cutting avoids the short-lasting barren look of clear cuts, it still leaves harvest debris and most owners who choose select harvest let the pines regenerate naturally from seeds. Marchinton says while the cost is not as much to re-establish pines this way, too often the pines are as thick as the hairs on a dog's back or there's not enough pine seedlings. So, consistency is hard to obtain. Forester Billy Humphries of Jeffersonville has noticed that clear cuts which are replanted with pines allowing adequate spacing often grow much faster than naturally regenerated pines.

Select cutting most often impacts property the same as clear cutting discussed above but leaves some mast producing trees which will drop acorns. This seems to lessen the apprehensions of timber harvesting among some property owners, especially among those concerned about wildlife. Select cutting also leaves a few trees to lean a ladder stand on and is generally thought to be more appealing to the eye. However, by cutting the largest, fastest growing trees you may be leaving smaller, slower growing and inferior trees to reseed the pines. This is not a simple topic so regarding timber harvest aspects, landowners should discuss their options with a knowledgeable forester before making an informed decision.

Surprisingly on Marchinton's own property, which is split equally between pines and hardwoods, he finds that he spends more time hunting in the pines than the hardwoods.

"Acorns are great food for the deer but when there's lots of acorns on the ground, the deer can be hard to pin point as far as location goes. So, I find myself hunting more in the pines than the hardwoods because I have a better chance of seeing the deer," he says.

The bottom line is that although clear cuts are ugly, this is just a temporary condition and better days lie ahead. Forests are dynamic, ever changing "natural factories" and clear cuts provide a diversity of habitat for wildlife and good browse for deer and turkeys, especially in conjunction with other adjacent properties which may be managed differently.

If you're sitting on a good deer hunting lease you should think hard before you abandon it due to a pending clear cut. Other valuable properties

are becoming difficult to locate, so you must ask yourself which is better, a bird in the hand or a bird in the bush? While clear cutting causes a temporary set- back in deer hunting prospects, if the hunting was good before the cut, it'll soon be good again. On WMA'S, timber will always be cut and thinned, so take it in stride!

A nice buck checks out his scrape during the night.

CHAPTER 11

WILD RUSSIAN BOARS OF OAKY WOODS WITH BOBBY TUGGLE

Oaky Woods is home to a large population of wild boar, but the wild boar in Oaky Woods WMA are special! Whereas all other wild hogs in Georgia originated as domestic stock gone wild, or" feral", the wild hogs in Oaky Woods have some true Russian Boar bloodlines due to a stocking of this true wild strain back in 1977 by Bobby Tuggle of Perry. These original Russian Boar have since interbred with the existing feral wild hogs, but the Wild Russian traits, (golden hairs around the mouth, smaller front shoulder, larger rear hams, taller thick black main hairs, bigger tusks) are still visible today, although diminished over time. Hunters from all over the United States come to Houston County to hunt these unique sporting trophies. The following story, which originally appeared in the February 1988 edition of Georgia Sportsman Magazine, written by the author, provides insight to the wild boar population in Oaky Woods and the surrounding area.

It seems that it was almost Bobby Tuggle's destiny to become known as the "Wild Hog Man of Middle Georgia." As a young man, this Perry, GA resident learned that his family coat of arms was emblazoned with the symbol of a wild boar. Later, while stationed in Fontainebleau, France, during the late 1950s, Tuggle became fascinated with wild boar hunting as it was practiced in Europe. He remembers "vast forests populated with wild boars and red stags which were hunted on horseback by royalty and the well-to-do."

"I was just a poor soldier and all I could do was watch and admire from a distance," he remembers. "But it was still quite a great sight to see the hunters all dressed in their red coats and blowing their hunting horns as they chased large, magnificent looking wild boars through the forest. Once the boars were bayed, they were dispatch with long spears."

Bobby Tuggle, on left, of Perry, with a huge, field dressed 530-pound boar killed in Middle Georgia. It was weighted on cotton scales in Hawkinsville. With him are Daniel Boone, Sr, right, and Daniel Boone, Jr

So while he watched and learned about European wild boar hunting from those that had practiced the sport for centuries, he swore to himself that someday, somewhere, he would eventually have the opportunity to hunt wild Russian boars. Many years later Tuggle leased a large tract of land just south of the Oaky Woods Wildlife Management Area (WMA) in Houston County and began an earnest search to locate wild boars to stock on the property. He finally found a pure strain of Russian wild boar in Ohio and traveled there to purchase nine Russian pigs from a dealer in exotic game. Two of these were boars; the balance was sows and gilts. Tuggle was very careful to observe all laws dealing with the interstate transport of the animals and kept them to breed in a yard pen on his leased property. Two years later, in 1977, he released 22 pigs into the surrounding forest and those pigs interbred with a small feral hog population (domestic pigs gone wild) which already existed in the area.

Since that time, the pigs have prospered and spread into other Middle Georgia areas, both naturally and at the hand of Tuggle and other wild pig enthusiasts.

Tuggle characterizes the Russian boar as a fierce game animal and a strong breeder. "They seem to more readily breed than feral hogs and now 10 years after the initial stocking, Middle Georgia probably has as many wild hogs as any other section of the country," says Tuggle. He estimates that 80 percent of the hogs he hunts today are predominately wild pigs. "I don't care anything about hunting a spotted feral pig. It's not sporting. But a wild Russian is another matter completely. You never know what to expect when hunting a wild pig. They are tremendously strong animals with huge shoulders, smaller hams and a large snout. They are swift runners, nearly as quick as a deer and regarded as one of the more intelligent wild animals. Although their sight and hearing are only average, their sense of smell is very good."

According to Tuggle, the Russian pigs are born striped like chipmunks "for protection in the wild." "Feral piglets are solid colored or spotted," he adds. But after a few months they (the Russian pigs) lose their stripes and become dark red. Then as they get older, they turn black or russet colored with gold or silver accent hairs protruding from their chins, jowls and underside, although these hairs may be visible on other parts of the body."

Tuggle, who has lived in Perry almost all his life, is an independent insurance salesman and (after working hours) an avid sportsman who primarily pursues wild hogs. His constant hunting companion is his son, Rob. Tuggle is a member of several hunting clubs and through friends, neighbors and farmers, he has accumulated access to thousands of acres of prime Middle Georgia wild hog habitat. Often landowners are glad to let Tuggle hog hunt on their property because the pigs damage crops and compete with deer fore available food. "A group of wild pigs can do considerable damage to crops like corn, peanuts or watermelons in a very short time," says Tuggle. "If not checked quickly they can wipe out a crop in a few days or weeks, depending on the size of the field."

The hogs hit at night, but Tuggle tracks them down with dogs during the day. Beginning in January after the deer season is over, Tuggle begins his wild hog season. "We don't want to interfere with the deer hunters and then also you have the woods nearly to yourself."

Tuggle usually meets his statewide circle of hog hunting friends at an all-night restaurant before daylight to organize the day's hunt. He is careful to limit both the number of hunters and dogs in the hunt because too many of either can make the hunt unmanageable. Usually the hunt is planned over breakfast and lots of hot coffee to insulate against the normally cold winter air that awaits the hunters. After receiving a number of strange looks from Interstate 75 travelers who don't know what to think about a large group of hunters in a restaurant at 5 a.m. and a parking lot full of restless dogs, the hunters load up their caravan of off-road vehicles and head to the predetermined destination.

That site can be thick woods, swampland, fields or a combination of all. Tuggle recommends that his friends and gusts come prepared for anything from swimming a creek or swamp to running a marathon with the dogs through some of the roughest territory imaginable; most of the time, his predictions come true. "If you're faint-hearted, wild hog hunting is not for you," says Tuggle.

"Part of the fascination of wild hog hunting is you never know what to expect" he continues, "both from the land you're on and the animal you're hunting. The European wild boar is a totally wild animal and unpredictable. They even look almost prehistoric in the forest. When they get mad, the hairs on their backs stand up and they flare and pop their tusks at you. They can be scare and dangerous. There is nothing else like them in our woods. A wild boar can rip open a dog or a man in a second, so great care must be taken while hunting them."

The dogs usually are released in the vicinity of fresh sign, but if none is found the hunters lead the dogs into areas the wild hogs may be frequenting, such as the edges of fields, creek bottoms, swamp perimeters or islands in swampy areas. Wild pigs often "hole up" in the thickest cover they can find, and once a dog smells the scent, it barks quietly and pursues the trail. The pig or group of pigs may be found in 50 yards or 5 miles; the hunters and dogs will stick with the fresh scent until the pigs are found.

Of course, the dogs don't wait for the hunters, so fast running on the part of the latter is the only way to keep up with the dogs. Once the dogs finally catch up with a pig they gang up and hold it until the hunters arrive. "Hopefully that's real soon or the pig will break loose or even worse. If it's a large wild boar with tusks, he can injure or kill the dogs," says Tuggle. The object is only to kill trophy wild boars which would be suitable for mounting. Smaller gilts, sows or small boars are wrestled down by the hunters and hog tied. Then, they are often released at the site, or another location where their presence is desired, kept breeding with other wild pigs.

"It takes a sure and quick hand to wrestle down a fighting mad wild pig and it's got to be done as rapidly as possible. It takes skill and experience to do it right, with safety always foremost in mind. And it usually helps if the dogs keep the pig distracted."

Tuggle and his hunting friends have caught approximately 150 wild pigs in the last four years, of which only about 30 were killed. He rates pigs over 250 pounds with good Russian characteristics as trophy animals. Pigs in this weight class have to be dispatched as quickly as possible to avoid injury to the dogs or hunters.

Despite the inherent risks of wild pig hunting, Tuggle says he has never felt in any real danger, although his son and some other hunters have on occasion climbed trees to avoid charging pigs.

Tuggle recalls one recent occasion when a hunter didn't have time to climb a tree. "A friend who had never hunted wild hogs came down from Atlanta and we went out hunting that morning. The dogs latched onto a large pig and the fight ended up in a creek where the pig threw off and defeated the dogs. The pig quickly swam back onto dry land and charged at my friend. Acting instinctively, he fires his .357 magnum (which he later said seemed very small at the time) at the pig as quickly as he could pull the trigger. I don't believe I've ever heard anyone shoot a revolver faster than he did that day. Anyway, he hit the pig three times and it collapsed right at his feet. He was shaken by the incident and said 'Mr. Tuggle, you never told me that these pigs would get me!'"

But it's that excitement that thrills Tuggle and his circle of hog hunters.

"Dogs are the key to this kind of hunting," Tuggle says. "They do most of the work and run the greatest risk of injury. Our vet bills this year alone is over $1,600, but we take good care of the dogs. Their job is to track and catch the wild pig by clamping down and holding on until the hunter arrives.

"Personally, I like the Catahoula breed, originating in France but bred in Louisiana for centuries for catching hogs. They're fairly strong, big and bark very little. It's important to have a silent tracking dog because if the pigs hear the dogs coming, they'll run off and you may have to chase them miles to catch 'em. The elk hound is another excellent breed that we use. Certain mixed breed dogs, such as bird dog and pit bull crosses, make good hog dogs because you wind up with the characteristics of the bird dog's scent abilities and the bulldog's tenacity. Other mixed breed canines may also make excellent hog dogs. Ability is what counts, not pedigree!"

As for the appropriate firearm for hog hunting, Tuggle feels that although deer class rifles would be good choices, they also are burdensome to carry the distances required for this type of hunting. He prefers to carry his .357 magnum Smith and Wesson (model 28 highway patrolman revolver) in a shoulder holster; his son, Rob, prefers a Ruger Blackhawk in .41 magnum caliber. The .44 magnum is another popular choice selected by Tuggle's hunting cronies.

"Powerful revolvers are adequate to get the job done," Tuggle feels, "and they are light and portable. In addition, when it's in the shoulder holster it leaves his hands free to handle the pig as necessary."

Baby wild pigs are striped like a chipmunk.

Tuggle's heard the arguments about an old wild boar being about as good to eat as an old leather shoe, but he disagrees. "Of course, pigs in the 80- 110-pound class usually provide excellent eating because it's young, tender meat but old boards usually are good too. If the pig is in poor condition, run down and skinny, it may be fit only for sausage or barbecue. But if the old boar's been eating well and has a good layer of body fat, you can pretty well be that he'll (taste) fine."

Tuggle also contends that wild pigs are quickly becoming one of Georgia's most popular big game animals. He says he has spoken with many hunters who would prefer to shoot a wild pig over a whitetail. "Wild pigs are often referred to as Georgia's other pig game and there's a lot of interest in hunting them. Their range is spreading. They can be hunted year-round and they provide outstanding sport."

While the "wild hog man of Middle Georgia" is enthusiastic about the status and future of the wild pig in Georgia, the Georgia Department of Natural Resources (DNR) has no concentrated interest in them. (The DNR considers them non-game animals, property of the landowner.) Ken Grahl, wildlife biologist for the Middle Georgia region, speculated that the drainage systems of the Ocmulgee and Oconee rivers in Middle Georgia might have a wild pig population of 10 per square mile. But he said his figure was only a guess. According to Grahl, several of the region's WMAs, including Oaky Woods, Ocmulgee, Beaver Dam, Horse Creek, Muskhogean and Chichsawhatchee have "decent" wild hog populations. But populations also exist in South Georgia, especially in the vicinity of the coast and also in the North Georgia mountains. Tuggle believes that the state may take more interest in wild hogs if hunter interest continues to grow, yet still feels that wild pigs should keep their current classification as non-game animals.

Tuggle is sold on the merits of wild hog hunting and every chance he gets he's loading up the dogs to hit the woods in pursuit of that "Ol' big boar that would make you quiver in your boots." His largest wild pig to date weighed 500 pounds and was taken in Pulaski County. He's hoping that enormous tusker has a big brother still wandering the forests of Middle Georgia.

That hope belies the outward appearance of Tuggle. He is a quiet, intelligent, unassuming person and doesn't appear to fit the mold of a rough and ready hog hunter. Yet underneath the quiet demeanor is a tough individualist who relishes the challenges of the sport. From the comfort of his insurance office, he carries out the tasks of his civilized job; but the bear rug and mounted trophies of wild boars, whitetails and ducks and that glimmer in his eye hint that he'd rather be in another time and another place.

But if Bobby Tuggle can't be in Europe chasing wild boars on horseback, the beautiful outdoors and wild boars of Middle Georgia will do just fine. (Update- It is against current state law to move or relocate wild pigs)

CHAPTER 12

PEACH STATE'S BEST BETS FOR WILD HOGS

The loud squeal of the wild pig in the thick bushes right in front of me perked my ears up to full attention. I doubted that they had caught my scent as the wind was favorable. It sounded more like they were fighting over an acorn or perhaps over the affections of a nearby sow, but with wild boar's hunters need to exercise caution. I recalled back many years ago that a cantankerous big boar had attacked a horse in a pasture near Augusta, severely wounding it. Also, while hunting boars with dogs, I have seen hunters chased around trees and the dogs cut up by the boar's sharp tusks. But normally when confronted by a hunter in a usual hunting situation, the wild pig knows his best plan of survival is a quick escape. Thus, as I moved as silently as I could toward the wild pigs, I carefully searched ahead of me for any sign of movement as I eased along an old deer path. Soon I saw a big black animal moving through the bushes. I put my scope on it to make absolutely sure it was a wild pig and not a black bear as they both were common on Oaky Woods WMA, where I was hunting. As the critter walked into a small opening, I saw that it was a jet- black boar weighing approximately 175 pounds. I only had about two seconds to shoot before the boar would be back in the thick bushes, so as soon as I put the scope on his heart area I pulled the trigger on my 50 caliber CVA black powder rifle. Soon I followed a good blood trail into a thick kudzu bramble and after crawling on my hands and knees for 30 yards, I found him piled up, stone dead, waiting for me. But the thrill of the hunt was not over yet.

After a few pictures, I had pulled out my knife to do the cleaning chore, when I heard another pig squeal about a 100 -yards away. I thought to myself, "the cleaning job can wait." In about 10 minutes I had another 50 – 75-pound sow on the ground, thus I had a very productive day! Of course, on a normal day it is a lot of hunting and very little shooting, so I was due for a good day. Although wild pigs are classified by the Georgia Department of Natural Resources as non-game animals due to their "domestic gone wild" heritage they are enthusiastically pursued by a multitude of Georgia hunters. These sportsmen hunt wild hogs for the challenge and diversity they offer in the woods and then later the good eating they provide on the table.

Domestic hogs were first brought to Georgia by Desoto and other early visitors around the 1540's. Because it was expensive to feed hogs, early settlers into Georgia often allowed the animals to freely roam the countryside in search of acorns or other nature provided grub. The settlers often provided supplemental feed and water to prevent the animals from wandering off too far. Hogs were also allowed into harvested fields to feed on surplus grains. This practice became known as "hogging down a field." When more pork was needed for the smokehouse these semi-wild hogs were rounded up. However, many hogs became independent minded and became totally self- sufficient in the woods, either by chance or being left behind when families moved because they could not be located in the woods. These hogs quickly reverted back to the feral "domestic gone wild" state and multiplied in remote sections of the state. To make the situation more interesting, these feral hogs have been interbred with truly wild Russian boars in the mountains and central areas of Georgia. Regardless of the lineage however, wild hogs are an exciting animal to hunt. Today, huntable populations primarily exist in the north Georgia mountains and along the lowlands of the Ocmulgee, Oconee, Ogeechee and Savannah Rivers. Wild pigs are highly adaptable to Georgia's woodlands and now occupy a majority of the state, Except for a wide spread of territory that stretches from above Atlanta to the state line near Columbus. Put your finger just about anywhere else on the map and wild pigs will be somewhere close by, usually concentrated in remote areas along mountains, damp rivers, swamps, creeks or our barrier islands.

Wild pigs may be hunted year- round on private properties with any deer, bear, turkey or small game firearm. On state WMA's and National Forest lands, wild hogs may be taken with archery equipment during archery deer season, with deer firearms during firearms deer season, with turkey firearms during turkey season and with small game weapons during small game season from August 15 – February 28. They can also be hunted with deer weapons on WMA's after the bobcat season opens, usually in December. So if you are bobcat hunting and happen to see a wild pig, you can take it. There also may be some special hunts for wild pigs on WMA's, so be sure to check the regulations for updates on an annual basis.

Among Georgia's "big three," which are bear, deer and wild pigs, the wild pigs provide an excellent hunting opportunity for those willing to go after them, especially during the early or late small game seasons on WMA's. The two wild hogs taken at the beginning of this story were shot on August 15th, the opening day of small game season. I took another nice 125 - pound boar during the March turkey season on Oaky Woods with my CVA black powder rifle. This is addition to the hunting opportunities I find available during the statewide archery and firearms deer season. But where can you find your wild pig in Georgia? Let's take a quick look at the best hunting locations on our WMA's.

Steve Gothenour shot this large wild boar in Macon County

Starting in Northeast Georgia, our biologist Scott Frazier says that the Chattahoochee and Chestatee WMAs contain good huntable wild hog populations, especially where Lumpkin, Union and White counties converge. The late frost this last spring damaged some soft and hard mast foods, but hopefully enough natural foods survived that the wild hogs won't be too negatively impacted, says Frazier. For the best hunting, he suggests hunters concentrate their efforts along lowland streams, bog areas and near food plots. Some hogs may also be found on War Woman WMA along major creeks and small feeder streams.

John Trussell harvested this small wild pig on Flat Creek PFA near Perry. During small game season, he often hunts with a black powder rifle for the first shot, then follows up with a 22 mag when necessary.

In Northwest Georgia, DNR biologist Adam Hammond says the region has a low density of wild hogs. The best places to find them are on Cohutta, Rich Mountain and Pine Log WMA's, with a few on Johns Mountain. In these areas, "the hogs are widely scattered, and a hunter would have to do some work to find them." He says a wise hunter would scout to find good food sources, like a group of oak trees dropping acorns or near a food plot of small grains with a good water source near- by.

In Central to West Georgia, DNR biologist Kevin Kramer would guide wild hog hunters to Ocmulgee and Oaky Woods WMAs which have good populations of wild pigs. On Ocmulgee, the majority of the pigs are located in area one, which is the most southern section of the WMA around and behind the check station, followed by area two.

Some hogs are scattered throughout the WMA, all the way to the north and along Richland Creek. On Oaky Woods, Kramer suggests scouting along both Big and Little Grocery Creeks that run through the center of the WMA and dump into the Ocmulgee River. Look for concentrations of acorns on the creek ridges and around the food plots for feeding pigs. He says more hogs are also showing up on Clybel WMA (Charlie Elliot). Hunters should also check out the wild hog quota hunt on Bond Swamp National Wildlife Refuge.

In Southwest Georgia, DNR biologist Brandon Rutledge says "more and more hogs are showing up each year" which is good news for hunters. But bad news for biologists that must contend with competition for limited food sources and damage to brush hog blades from mounds of dirt pushed up by rooting hogs. The best WMA for hogs in this area is Chickasawhatchee and Rutledge suggests that hunters work around the edges of the swamp and stalk into the areas of high ground that jut into water where the pigs forage. The WMA hosts several special hog hunts where deer firearms may be used, check the regs for full details.

In South Central Georgia, DNR biologists Greg Waters and Chris Baumann would guide hunters to Riverbend, Beaverdam, Big Hammock, Horse Creek and Bullard Creek WMAs for the best chance at a wild hog. All these areas have good populations along the Ocmulgee River and nearby drainages. Last year, for example, Beaverdam produced 32 hogs and Riverbend turned in 22 during the deer hunts. The big surprise for Big Hammock, where 47 hogs were killed, but many more were taken here and on all state WMAs during the small game hunts that are not reported or documented. Down in the Waycross area, DNR biologist Greg Nelms says the hogs are scattered but a few can be found on Dixon WMA and occasionally a few wander across Grand Bay WMA, some of the area burned during the summer which has recently greened up will draw in some wild hogs.

One of the largest populations of wild hogs occurs along the Georgia coast, particularly on the barrier islands, DNR biologist Ed Van Otteren, who works out of the Brunswick office, says they have "a bunch of wild hogs" and encourages hunters to come out hunting and take a few home with them. He suggests the quota hunt on Ossabaw Island as one of the best to apply for, but Sapelo Island has several open deer archery and small game hunts that offer good opportunity for the last-minute hunter.

There are several federal land areas along the coast that host opportunities to bag a wild hog., Among them are Blackbeard Island NWR, Cumberland Island NS, Harris Neck NWR, Savannah River NWR, and Wassaw Island. Some hunts are quota, and some are open sign-in hunts. For complete information on the application deadlines, phone numbers, hunt fees and other regulations, refer to the current Georgia 2007-08 hunting seasons and regulations booklet. It takes a little planning and preparation to hunt the coastal islands, but they offer a good chance to take home the bacon!

John Trussell harvested these large wild pigs on land close to Oaky Woods

CHAPTER 13

DEALING WITH MERAUDERS IN OUR MIDST

As I closed the distance to my target, I was both excited and cautious. It was ten pm in the evening, pitch black dark and just a little spooky as we eased across the field to intercept the unwanted guests in our midst. However, I was comforted by the fact that I was well armed and equipped for the anticipated encounter. In my hands was a DPMS AR-10 type, semi auto rifle in caliber 308, topped with a 6-power night vision scope that allowed me to see my target, while I remained basically invisible. No, I was not in some foreign land, fighting insurgents, but in a farmer's field, fighting invaders. We had caught the marauding wild animals "in the act" of destroying private property and it was time to bring them to justice.

Usually striking in the small hours of the early morning, wild pigs attack anything eatable like planted peanuts, corn, or any type of vegetable and water melons, resulting in huge financial loses for land owners. Sometimes they root up tubers, nut grasses and grubs in open fields and freshly planted pine trees, doing considerable damage to Georgia forestry, as they leave large potholes and mounds of dirt. Also, they compete with deer and turkey for food sources as they vacuum up vast amounts of acorns. The main solution is to remove the offending wild pigs, but the task is not easy. This is a job for professionals!

Ron Pinkston, Troy Day, Kyle Warnke and John Trussell had a good night busting wild pigs in a watermelon field

Jager Pro, which means professional hunter, was established in May of 2006 by Rod Pinkston, of Columbus, Georgia to help reduce the economic and environmental damage caused by wild hogs in the state of Georgia. Rod explains that," Our primary mission is to provide farmers and plantation owners with innovative wild hog management through the implementation of military-grade thermal devices. We accomplish this mission by offering hunting clients the ultimate tactical boar hunting experience and adventure. We also donate much of our harvest to provide nutritious meals for families in need. So Jager Pro brings together farmers and land owners with a specific need to eliminate wild pigs with supervised hunters who desire a unique hunting experience. Farmers and land owners are not charged for the services of Jager Pro to remove wild pigs from their property, but hunters pay for the unique hunting opportunity to hunt wild pigs at night with night vision scopes. The hunters who accompany Rod are well briefed on the use of the weapon and equipment they carry, the procedure for the nights hunt and safety zones in the area. They also sign waivers of liability.

Pinkston's secondary mission is to equip farmers, plantation managers, hunters and state/federal wildlife professionals with long-range ear tag transmitters, electronic trapping devices and high-resolution infrared scopes to help solve human-wildlife conflicts. He applies his military experience, products and technology to wild hog management and seeks to be the premier hog control operator in the United States.

Bruce West, a farmer in Dooley County, examines damage to his watermelon crop from wild pigs. They can eat or destroy several hundreds of dollars of crop each night!

Rod Pinkston has earned his living as a Soldier during the past 24 years. He recently retired from the United States Army Marksmanship Unit's Olympic Shooting Team at Fort Benning, Georgia after his Soldiers won two gold medals at the 2008 Olympic Games in Beijing, China. He has also served as a Senior Field Editor with Boar Hunter Magazine, a member of the National Wildlife Control Operators Association and earned the coveted "Jagdschein" hunting European boars in Germany, Poland and the Czech Republic.

The hunt described above occurred on the evening of June 1, 2011. Rod Pinkston, Troy Day of Perry, owner of nightvisionhogcontrol.com, Kyle Warnke, a reporter for channel 41 NBC in Macon, and Bruce West, a large property farmer from Byromville, and I met near a large watermelon field in Dooley County to help eliminate a serious wild hog problem. Wild hogs had been raiding West's watermelon field every night and destroying hundreds of valuable melons with each visit. West said he had no doubt that the wild pigs could cost him thousands of dollars in lost income, thus it was time to meet the problem head on! So, we gathered in the late afternoon to wait on the wild pigs to come out after the sun set. We did not have to wait too long, as about 10 pm, Pinkston spotted, with his night vision scope, a large group of wild pigs out in the water melon field, at a range of about 200 yards. But the wind was wrong for an approach, so we had to walk around to another location and that took 30 minutes. But soon we were able to walk to within 50 to 100 yards of the group of 16 wild pigs who were busy busting and slurping up large numbers of water melons! Through our rifle night scopes, we could clearly see the pigs, which was amazing! We lined up, and on the count of three, we tried to shoot as many wild pigs as possible. The gun muzzle flashes were bright, the noise blasts were loud, and it was a little like being in a gun battle, but thankfully the pigs could not shoot back! We shot some of the bigger pigs quickly, but many were small pigs, making them tough targets and the shooting was over quickly as the pigs ran for a nearby corn patch, where they disappeared. A quick count of the dead wild pigs, that would never destroy another watermelon, was four. We hoped for more, but since we only had about two seconds to shoot, we were pleased with the results. On an average night, Pinkston's hunters kill 3-7 wild pigs, but sometimes they kill many more. Pinkston schedules hunts all over southwest Georgia, and Troy schedules hunts in middle Georgia, so contact them if you want to get rid of wild pigs on your property. But shooting wild pigs is not the only way to eliminate them.

Ron Pinkston helps Kyle Warnke adjust the night vision scope on an AR 10, 308 caliber rifle.

Trapping is a very effective control method for removing large numbers of feral hogs; especially juveniles, says Pinkston. Late winter (December-March) is usually an optimum opportunity when hogs are searching for new food sources after the fall mast crops of acorns and hickory nuts are eaten. Traps have emerged in a variety of door designs, materials, sizes and shapes. As in hunting, there are certain methods and procedures which are more effective than others.

"The most effective design in our research", says Pinkston," has been a large corral trap using six livestock panels, an automatic feeder and a 12- foot gate closed by a remote- control device. This method of trapping allowed us to capture entire sounder groups (family units) with the push of a button. Timers were set to broadcast feed every day at the exact same time. Game cameras captured video footage of hogs entering the trap area for two weeks to gather data. We then sat downwind of corral trap to observe feeding activity based on gathered data".

"We make an educated decision when to close the door", says Pinkston. "Sometimes, there was only a short period of time when all hogs were inside the trap during 20 minutes of feeding. This method is similar to hunting except you are pushing the button on a remote- control device catching the entire group instead of pulling the trigger on a rifle and harvesting one animal. This approach was our most effective trapping method and demonstrated whole sounder removal every time". Keep in mind that this hunt was on private property and wild hogs cannot be hunted at night on WMA's. Check annually for new Georgia DNR regulations.

CHAPTER 14

WINTER IS A GREAT TIME FOR SMALL GAME HUNTING

Today about 75% of all hunting is deer hunting, but don't overlook the great small game hunting available in Oaky Woods and all over our fine state! Do you remember your first game animal taken with bow or gun? It is usually an event one never forgets, and it is a special memory that always harkens you back to a younger, simpler place in time. When I was about 10 years old, I had a Crossman pump up pellet gun that I had gotten for Christmas and soon squirrels were my chosen targets as they dug up seeds from my dad's garden and eat their weight in pecans every day, thus they ate into the family purse. They also tried to eat their way into the attic of our house and chewed on our plastic water hoses, thus they were not welcome or "persona non-grata" around my house. On the plus side they were very plentiful, were elusive targets and once cleaned and fried, darn good eating!

It was shortly after I got my pellet gun that I spotted a squirrel in our back yard, and as I approached, it scurried up a small oak tree and seemed to disappear! But soon I spotted a few hairs from its tail as it laid flat against a branch, and every time I moved around for the shot, it slid around to the other side of the tree. I thought, "Darn it, how can I outsmart this squirrel"? Then I had a eureka moment! Having a brain just slightly bigger than the squirrels, I quickly figured out that if I threw a small limb to the other side of the tree, it might think that I had moved, and show itself for a shot. Trying that technique, I was soon looking at a target big enough for a shot and a well place pellet to the head brought the squirrel tumbling to the ground. I was one proud hunter! As I proudly carried by prize to show my parents, my mom's brief comment was," that's great son, now go clean it, don't expect me to do it"! Thus, my first cleaning was sort of a hatchet - job on the squirrel, but it did not seem to mind, and I put it in the Refrigerator. A couple of nights later at supper, my mom announced with a smile on her face and a wink in my direction, that we were having fried squirrel and chicken and I was glad to have put some meat on the table. Insert your own "first game animal story here" and I'll bet it is more special than mine! Now let's get to hunting! Although deer hunting gets a lot of press time, small game hunting in Georgia is nothing short of outstanding! In this article we will focus on squirrels, rabbits, quail and will start on the proper loads for each species.

Although there are several gauges of shotguns, I have always been partial to the 12-gauge semi -auto with screw in chokes. It's very versatile and throws the most lead, but a smaller gauge, if you're accurate with it, can be just as effective. Number 6 shot is very good for both rabbits and squirrels out to 40 yards when using a modified choke. For quail, the shots may be closer and number 8 shot is generally preferred. For quail, use an improved cylinder choke for close in shooting that you might find at a quail plantation. For quail in more open areas, a modified choke that holds a tighter pattern, is a better choice.

For Rabbits the best places to hunt are normally cutovers with vegetation in the early stages of regeneration with lots of brambles and briars. Private properties with little hunting pressure with usually reveal the most rabbits. But don't overlook public hunting areas.

A fox squirrel tries to hide on a tree limb

Down in central Georgia, both Oaky Woods and Ocmulgee WMA's offer pretty good rabbit hunting, says Kevin Kramer, Regional Supervisor Biologist with the Ft Valley office. Thick, cut over areas usually offer the best cover for rabbits, says Kramer, and just driving around the WMA's will quickly reveal some likely areas to explore, like the cut over across from the cell phone tower on the main road going to the Oaky Woods check station. Another spot is the cutover behind the school bus body, shown on the WMA map. Many of the upland pine areas have been thinned in the last two years and as the under- story vegetation develops, the rabbits will move back in, says Kramer. On 17,370-acre Ocmulgee WMA try area six, south of Highway 96 or area five off of Longstreet Church road. Bobby Bond, DNR's rabbit Biologist, says rabbits are in normal numbers and hunters should have average to good success with a little work. "Look for that successional habitat that is 3-5 years old and the rabbits will be there, but you might have to work at finding them".

Rabbit Hunter Bill Bethune, left, often brings new hunters into the sport. To his right are Brandon, Jack and Ava Trussell and Walker Bethune. Bill often hunts on WMA's, like Oaky Woods

When walking around in warm weather, be on the lookout for poisonous snakes like this diamondback rattler that was spotted in Oaky Woods. Usually, I leave all snakes alone and most are non- poisonous.

In SW Georgia, region five, Julie Robbins, wildlife biologist says that Chichasawhatchee WMA is her top pick for rabbits. It has a good mix of uplands, oaks and water that holds good numbers of rabbits. Other choices might be Albany Nursery, River Creek or Elmodel. Greg Nelms, area six biologist from Fitzgerald, says that although the flatwoods of South Georgia can be hard to hunt, his top choice would be Dixon Memorial Forest WMA as some areas have been burned over and are regenerating good browse for rabbits. "Look for that successional habitat that is 3-5 years old and the rabbits will be there, but you might have to work at finding them. Now let's take a quick look at squirrel hunting

Imagine if you will a game animal that is not only under-hunted but is very abundant all over the state and the open season is almost seven months long! In addition, the daily limit is a generous 10 per day and they can be hunted with both shotguns and rifles, as well as with or without dogs. It would seem as though squirrel hunting offers something for most hunters, and it does. Squirrels are also a fine game animal on which to train young hunters. Under the watchful eye of an adult, youngsters can develop the searching, patience, and stalking skills which are so important to all hunting activities. And because squirrels are so plentiful, a young hunter's chances of success are high. There's nothing like a few squirrels in the game bag and pleasant memories of the hunt to fuel a kid's desire to return to the woods. Back home, a mess of squirrel and dumplings will give the young hunter a wholesome meal that he can be proud to provide for the family. To get started, just head to any good woodlot with pretty of acorn and hickory nut trees and the squirrels will be there. If you can set still for about 10 minutes, the squirrels will reveal themselves and you're in business. I like to use a scoped 22 rifle for squirrel hunting, trying for head shots, but a young hunter will get better results with a shotgun. A single shot 410 makes a fine first gun. Now let's consider quail hunting, but where have all the quail gone?

Quail numbers have greatly decreased across Georgia

I used to have a great time quail hunting as a kid, but today I can hunt all day and be lucky to run across a single covey of quail. Biologists may point to modern farming methods, poor habitat, or too many predators like foxes, armadillos, bobcats and coyotes as reason for the decline. Too many ants may also be a factor too. Just drop a bread crumb on the ground anywhere in Middle to South Georgia and there are ants on it within a few minutes. A baby quail coming out of the shell had better get moving quick because something's trying to eat it! If I really want to have a great quail hunt, I head to one of Georgia's 94 quail plantations that specialize in planning the best quail hunting experience for Georgia sportsmen. You can count on having a great hunting trip with good friends and they put some great food on the table!

For great Quail hunting, try one of Georgia's Quail Plantations. Above, Leon Scott, left, John Trussell and Jimmy Jacobs quail hunt at Noontootla Farms Hunting club, near Blue Ridge, Georgia.

CHAPTER 15
COUGARS IN OAKY WOODS AND GEORGIA?

Are there any cougars in Georgia? Every year this writer gets a phone call from an outdoorsman who tell me they saw a cougar in Central Georgia and it looked like a very large black cat. I try to explain that it was probably a dark colored coyote, which constitutes about 10% of our local coyote population. When one of these dark color phase coyotes gets wet, which is often, they can look like a large cat, then we struggle to imagine what we saw! As we discuss this topic, let us differentiate between cougars and panthers.

The largest cat in the United States, and in fact the fourth largest cat in the world, is the mountain lion (*Puma concolor*) – also known as cougar, catamount, and in Florida, panther. Adult cougars are about 120-150 pounds, have tawny or light brown coats. With the exception of the endangered Florida panther population and a few solitary and long-distance travelers, they live in the western part of the country. Cougars have been hunted for centuries and are one of the best-studied animals on the planet, yet *there has never been a cougar documented displaying melanism, or black color.*

This cougar, among a population of only about 200, roams around south Florida. Photo by Larry Richardson, US Fish and Wildlife Service

Melanism is a genetic variation that results in excess pigmentation turning the coat entirely black, and this variation just isn't part of a cougar's genetic make-up. To date, there has never been such thing as a black mountain lion. The only animals that legitimately fit the "black panther" description live in central and south America and are not found in the USA.

But have cougars ever lived in Georgia? We do know that in prehistoric times, cougars lived in Georgia and a native American head dress was excavated at the Ocmulgee Indian Mounds in Macon that had a cougar jaw in it. Of course, there is no way to tell if the cougar jaw was local or a far -off trade item, but early America settlers often reported cougar sightings. These cougars were killed whenever they were found, and no wild cougar has been documented in Georgia in modern times, except one!

Bobcats are a top predator in Oaky Woods

In November 2008, one of the Georgia sighting incidents was proven true when a deer hunter on public Corps of Engineers land near

West Point Lake in Troup County shot and killed a 140-pound panther that measured 7 feet, 4 inches from nose to tail.

The cat was examined at the Southeastern Cooperative Wildlife Disease Study in Athens, Ga., where experts found the panther to be healthy and well fed, with scuffed pads on all four feet. Such characteristics are consistent with a panther reared in captivity, not in the wild, and more than 1000 people in Florida have captive cougar permits. But wildlife officials were in for a surprise when DNA tests on the cat proven it was wild!

It was examined at the Southeastern Cooperative Wildlife Disease Study in Athens. No microchips, tags, tattoos or other means of marking a captive animal turned up. According to Paul Souza, South Florida Ecological Services field supervisor, "Finding a Florida panther that far from southwest Florida is out of the ordinary, but male panthers, particularly younger ones, can travel great distances. While it's unusual for panthers to be seen that far north, it is not impossible for a young male to travel so far." It is very rare, but not impossible!

Also, the Feds occasionally consider the idea of relocating some Florida cougars. Some research has been done on the topic and it pops up from time to time

The federal wildlife managers say that to ensure the survival of panthers, they eventually will have to widen their range. Among the handful of other spots, the report names as most hospitable to the big cats is the more than 400,000-acre Okefenokee refuge, according to Mike Williams with Cox International and Rob Pavey, the outdoor writer for the Augusta Chronicle.

Coyotes are very common in Georgia, eat just about anything and take a heavy toll on all wildlife. US Fish and Wildlife photo.

According to the report, a limited experiment in the late 1980s and the first half of 1990s placed panthers from Texas near the Okefenokee refuge, and they appeared to adapt well. But at the end of the trial, they were removed. The report acknowledges that reintroducing the cats — which can reach 8 feet in length and weigh 140 pounds — is more challenging than simply finding suitable habitat.

"Although there appeared to be support for reintroduction among the general public, local landowners tended to oppose having panthers on their property," the report said.

Even though there are no plans for any reintroduction into Georgia, some residents in Folkston, which bills itself as "The Gateway to the Okefenokee," would rather not host the cats. Some residents recall that during the experimental release, there were several attacks on family pets and livestock. Some of the cats were killed, too. Such concerns aren't lost on wildlife managers, who say any reintroduction program will come only after extensive efforts to enlist public support.

"Public acceptance is the most important factor in any future recovery plan," said Paul Souza, a U.S. Fish and Wildlife Service field supervisor involved in the effort to save the animals. "We want to establish a track record of public-private partnership in South Florida that can be a model for reintroduction into other areas."

The panthers once ranged across the Southeast, a top predator feeding on deer, wild boar and other game.

But contact with colonial settlers proved deadly for the cats, which were hunted and shot by farmers protecting their livestock. The inexorable push of railroads, cities and highways into once wild forested areas also destroyed their habitat.

Listed by federal officials in the 1960s as endangered, they are considered one of the planet's species most at-risk for extinction. By the 1980s they were found only in a large swath of swampy land in South Florida including the Big Cypress National Preserve and Everglades National Park.

Their numbers had dwindled to an estimated 20 to 30 animals, a population so low that researchers found newborns were beset by sterility, heart defects and other problems triggered by inbreeding.

In a desperate bid to stave off extinction, wildlife managers in 1995 brought in eight female Texas panthers, a closely related species, to broaden the genetic pool. The gamble paid off, and the panthers rebounded to about 100 to 120 cats today.

But the species' survival is far from assured. Male panthers require up to 200 square miles of territory each, and the current population already is straining the 3,500 square mile area they now inhabit.

Several long-running studies have led wildlife managers to conclude the best chance for survival is the reintroduction of the panthers to locations other than South Florida. Ideally, three populations in separate areas would give the cats their best shot.

"We're looking at the numbers we need for genetic viability, and we think it's about 240," said Souza. Georgia officials have participated in some of the panther research but have no official position on reintroduction.

"We don't want to see the species lost and will be willing to explore possibilities, but if you can't get the support of the people in the area it isn't viable," said Mike Harris, chief of the Non-Game Conservation Section of the state's Department of Natural Resources in speaking with Rob Pavey, a writer with the Augusta Chronicle.

In Folkston, news that the area might be considered as a relocation spot for the panthers has generated headlines in the local newspaper, with some residents expressing opposition. But others say they would welcome the chance to help save the species.

Although not specifically mentioned, it might be possible for Savannah River Site, which has 310 square miles of forested lands and plenty of river drainage, to be considered. The land is part of the panther's former home range—and has plenty of room for the cats to roam, says Rob Pavey.

Ken Warren, who works in the U.S. Fish & Wildlife Service Ecological Services Office in Vero Beach, Fla., told Pavey that scientists are already looking at as many as nine areas that might be suitable for reintroduction programs. But moving panthers into new areas is more complicated than it sounds.

The process would require a lot of public hearings and may stir opposition from landowners and the public. The eastern cougar was common across the entire south before they were killed off or simply died out as their habitat vanished.

Jack Mayer, a researcher, author and scientist at the U.S. Department of Energy's Savannah River National Laboratory, said there is certainly enough land at SRS to accommodate panthers. "Size-wise, it's 310 square miles out here," he said. "You have a nice, big chunk of real estate, but it's likely these animals would move in a high-use corridor system. So even if you introduce them out here, they might use the area, but I'd guarantee they will move all up and down the river. They don't sit tight."

Dr. Mayer's decades as a research scientist included a stint in Florida, where he worked on a 175,000-acre ranch where eight Florida panthers were known to reside. He was most impressed by their ability to escape detection. "For two years, with eight panthers on the property off and on, we never found any scats, and we only found two sets of tracks the whole time," he said. "It's like they walk a foot above the ground and they don't leave any sign."

The concept of releasing Florida panthers into their former habitat has been studied off and on for a long time, he said, recalling on experiment in the mid-1990s in which a group of Texas panthers was released in northern Florida.

"They went and got a bunch of Texas cougars and had them sterilized. They tied the tubes on females and vasectomized the males—and let them go," he said. "They wanted to see what happened. They didn't want to risk taking the precious genetic stock out of south Florida and risk having something happen to them. The wandering cats did exactly what scientists thought they would do: they wandered.

"Some ended up getting killed, and some disappeared and all they found was a radio collar," he said. "One big male moved onto a goat farm near Jacksonville, and the farmer kept running him off, and it moved on toward Jesup. Then I guess he got hungry and moved back to the goat farm, so they went and picked him up."

One of the most interesting cougar journeys of the experiment involved a big male that wandered into Georgia. Over a period of several months during summer and fall of 1995—it crossed the entire state and ended up in Burke County. It then meandered south toward Statesboro before returning to Burke County, then followed the Brier Creek drainage into McDuffie County, where it lingered for a week near Thomson.

Eventually, it made its way to the Clarks Hill Wildlife Management Area near Thurmond Lake, where biologists recaptured it the following February and returned it to Florida, as reported by Pavey.

What was most interesting about that particular panther's voyage was the fact that it covered so much ground–and it never generated a single reported sighting.

The ability of the panther—or cougar or mountain lion, as they are also called—to move undetected has fueled a perennial debate over whether we already have them wandering around in our forests and swamps.

The official response from both the Georgia Wildlife Resources Division and the S.C. Department of Natural Resources is that there has never been a documented wild cougar found in either state in modern times. But there are plenty of reported sightings. Each year, mainly during the fall hunting seasons, the two states receive or investigate as many as 75 cougar reports, all of which have been inconclusive. Georgia Outdoor News magazine had a photo contest in 2015 where outdoorsmen where to turn in their best trail camera shots of a panther. After several months, they did declare a winner, but it looked like a bobcat to me!

Florida panthers belong to the last subspecies of Puma left in the eastern United States. Once they prowled throughout the Southeast. Now only 100 to 120 remain in south Florida, their range less than 5 percent of what it once spanned.

So, will reports of cougar sightings increase in Georgia? Probably not, unless they are re-introduced into the South Georgia swamp. This writer thinks it would be a good thing to bring cats to the Okeefenokee refuge, once their natural range, but public support is critical. That support might grow if local farmers are compensated for any cougar damage to their livestock, but the feds will undoubtedly consider that factor in any plan to reintroduce cougars. At this point in time there are no plans to move cougars out of Florida. Thus, it remains highly unlikely that you'll ever see a cougar in Georgia, but as the 2008 cougar killed near Lagrange proves- never say never!

CHAPTER 16
OAKY WOODS, ONCE AT THE BOTTOM OF THE OCEAN, HAS RICH GEOLOGIC PAST

Woods Wildlife Management area is peppered with ancient paleontology fossils like sand dollars and whale bones. Where did they come from? For background during the Cretaceous period (145 to 65.5 million years ago), the climate was much warmer than it is today, and tropical conditions existed in Georgia. No glaciers existed at the poles, and as a result, sea level was much higher than it is at present. The Atlantic Ocean covered southeastern Georgia inland as far as present-day Macon, Columbus, and Augusta, and left marine sediments containing mollusk shells, sharks' teeth, bits of turtle shell, and the occasional dinosaur bone. Dinosaurs roamed Georgia during the Cretaceous and sometimes floated out to sea after they died. The remains of such dinosaurs as the duck-billed hadrosaurs and the ferocious carnivore Albertosaurus, a close relative of Tyrannosaurus rex, are found in Late Cretaceous rocks (65 to 100 million years old) These fossils have been found near Columbus and Rome, Georgia, but not in central Georgia. The Cretaceous ended with the extinction of the dinosaurs, possibly as a result of an asteroid impact or a combination of natural causes.

John Trussell holds two sand dollars from an exposed limestone ridge along Big Grocery Creek in Oaky Woods WMA in Houston County. The sand dollars are about 32 million years old. Please do not try to dig fossils from the cliffs!

From the Late Cretaceous period to the Middle Eocene epoch of the Paleogene period (about 40 to 100 million years ago), large quantities of kaolinite, a white alumino-silicate clay resembling chalk, were deposited in middle Georgia. (Kaolin is mined for use in the manufacture of glossy paper, plastic, rubber, paints, ceramics, and other products. Georgia is the world's leading producer of kaolin.) This clay derives from the weathering of feldspar, a mineral found in Piedmont rocks. The clay was transported by streams and deposited in deltas, estuaries, and coastal marshes.

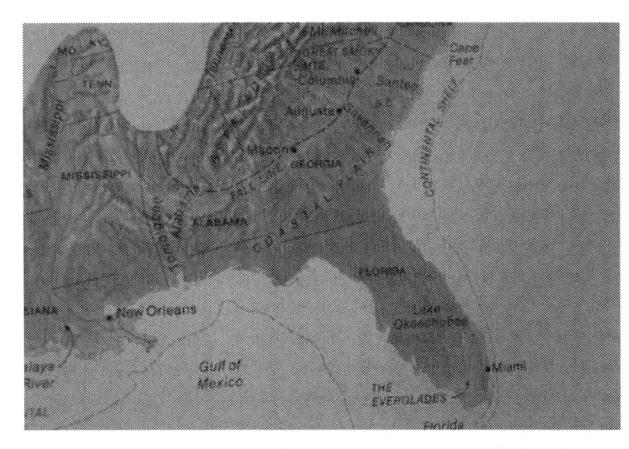

The fall line, which runs across central Georgia, marks an ancient high-level sea shore. The continental Shelf, 75 miles off the Georgia coast, marks the low water mark for the ocean during the last ice age that ended 12,000 years ago

Marine deposits associated with kaolin, including abundant limestone, indicate that the Coastal Plain was flooded by a warm, shallow sea. This sea was inhabited by mollusks, sand dollars, foraminifera, bryozoans, and an early whale with hind legs (38 to 41 million years ago), an evolutionary remnant from an ancestor that walked on land. This is the period from which our Oaky Woods sand dollars come into being.

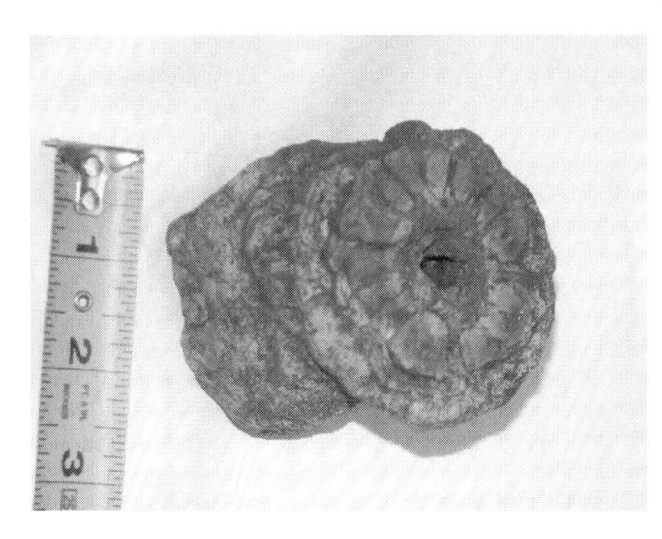

John Trussell found this piece of coral in Oaky Woods.

A dramatic event occurred about 35 million years ago during the Eocene era, when an asteroid or comet struck the Chesapeake Bay region of Virginia. The impact shattered and melted the rocks at the point of impact, forming a crater, 90 kilometers in diameter and ejecting droplets of molten rock, which flew through the air for hundreds of kilometers. The molten rock cooled to form coin-sized, translucent, green glassy stones known as tektites, some of which landed in the sea covering east-central Georgia.

The climate cooled dramatically near the end of the Eocene, and during the remainder of the Cenozoic era, glaciers began to grow and the worldwide sea level dropped. The seas receded from Georgia, and sediments derived from the erosion of the Appalachian Mountains and the Piedmont built eastward. Sediments were deposited at a thickness of more than 5,000 meters, or 5 kilometers, in the Coastal Plain area and thickened toward the southeast.

Neogene Period

This small waterfall in Oaky Woods and the rocky terrain is very unusual in Houston County and helps to make Oaky Woods a special place!

Glaciers periodically covered much of northern North America during the Pleistocene epoch (1.8 million years ago to the present), although Georgia remained ice-free. The seas alternately flooded and retreated from the land along the coast as the glaciers advanced and receded. During peak glacial episodes, sea level was about 100 to 120 meters lower than at present, and the coast was out near the edge of the continental shelf. Between glaciations, sea level stood as much as 50 meters above present levels. Sea-level high stands are marked by beach ridges. Beaches were dominated by white quartz sand, but during times of rising sea level or higher wave energy, concentrations of black sands, rich in such heavy minerals as ilmenite, zircon, rutile, epidote, sillimanite, staurolite, magnetite, tourmaline, and kyanite, formed on the beaches. Some of these heavy mineral sands are present in Pleistocene beach ridges near the Okefenokee Swamp and contain valuable economic deposits of titanium.

This Ancient whale, adorudon serratus, is the same type found in Oaky Woods. This one is in Macon's Arts and Sciences Museum.

During the Pleistocene, Georgia was inhabited by mammals not seen today, including mastodons, mammoths, elephants, camels, bison, tapirs, and giant ground sloths up to 6 meters tall. The climate was arid at times during the Pleistocene. About 20,000 years ago, rivers dried up and strong winds from the west blew the river sand into large dunes. Pleistocene sand-dune fields remain along the east side of several rivers, including the Flint, Ohoopee, and Canoochee.

When the last ice age ended about 12,000 years ago, the oceans were about 50-75 miles further out than they are now. The water started to rise and has been rising, but not constantly, since that time. The National Weather Service estimates that the oceans are now rising about 1/8 inch per year and over time this rise, in the next few hundred years, will cause severe flooding in coastal areas. Many coastal islands are only a few feet above sea level. Time will tell how much the oceans will rise and the only constant on earth is change!

Alligators are common along the Ocmulgee River in Oaky Woods- This one lives at the Go Fish Center in Perry.

CHAPTER 17
THE DAY THE HEAVENS RAINED FIRE ON CENTRAL GEORGIA

About 35 million years ago a meteor streaked across the horizon and the sky glowed as though it was lit by 100 suns! During the Eocene era, an asteroid or comet struck the Chesapeake Bay region of Virginia. The impact shattered and melted the rocks at the point of impact, forming a crater, 90 kilometers in diameter and ejecting droplets of molten rock, which flew through the air for hundreds of kilometers. The molten rock cooled to form coin-sized, translucent, green glassy stones known as tektites, some of which landed in the sea covering east-central Georgia. The word Tektite comes from the Greek word Tektos, which means molten. Many of these tektites landed in Bleckley, Dodge and surrounding counties and at least one was confirmed in Houston County.

Most people would not know a tektite if they saw one. I think I might have found one many years ago, in a field near Oaky Woods. But misplaced it before I could confirm it and it looked like a small, glassy rock. I currently have several tektites, but they were given to me by Hal Povenmire, a NASA scientist. They are now fairly common around the world, used for jewelry and you can buy them on E-bay or other sites. They are another part of our natural world and you may stumble across one day as you wonder around middle Georgia!

Although our local tektites are thought to have come from the Chesapeake Bay region, another meteor struck the Yucatan Peninsula about 66 million years ago and dug a crater that was 62 miles wide and 19 miles deep. All this occurred in less than one second! This is the event that wiped out 75 percent of live on earth, including the dinosaurs. The evidence for this event was discovered by oil scientists and today the Chicxulub crater is buried underground, filled in by erosion sediments.

The best book on this subject "Tektites, A Cosmic Enigma", was written by Hal Povenmire, a NASA scientist, who was the radio and tv voice of the space agency for many years. I had the good fortune to meet and talk with Hal several years ago at an archaeology event. The overwhelming consensus of Earth and planetary scientists is that tektites consist of terrestrial debris that was ejected during the formation of an impact crater.

During the extreme conditions created by an hypervelocity meteorite impact, near-surface terrestrial sediments and rocks were either melted, vaporized, or some combination of these and ejected from an impact crater. After ejection from the impact crater, the material formed millimeter- to centimeter-sized bodies of molten material, which as they re-entered the atmosphere, rapidly cooled to form tektites that fell to Earth to create a layer of distal ejecta hundreds or thousands of kilometers away from the impact site.

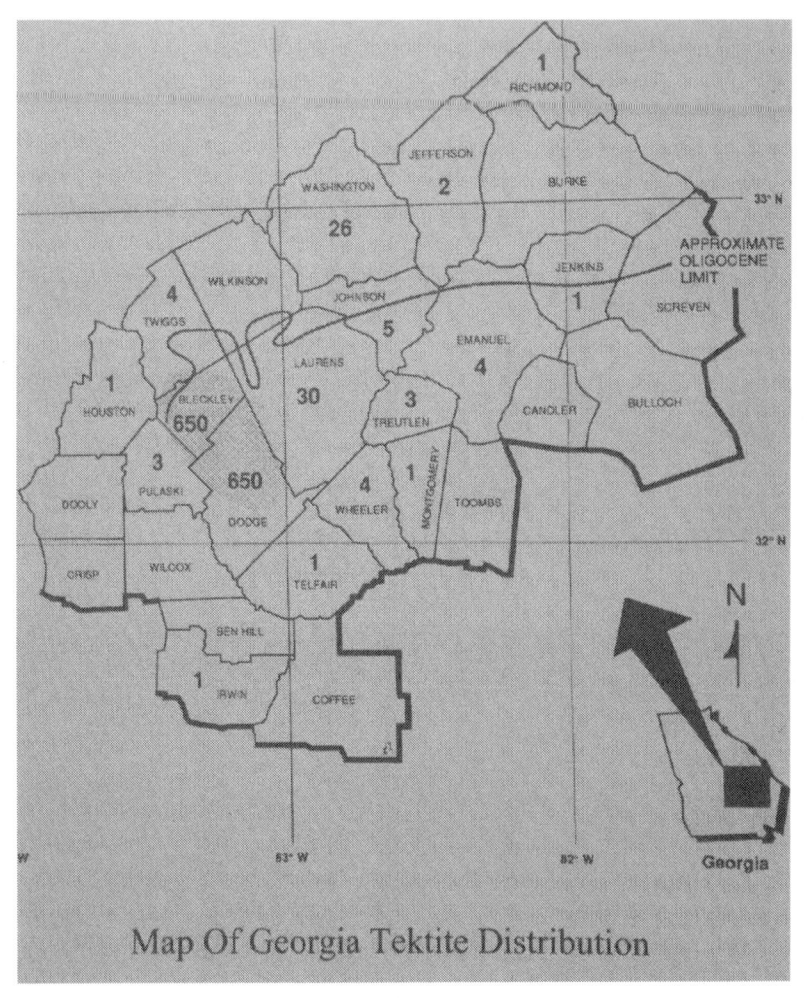

Map Of Georgia Tektite Distribution

This map shows the tektite distribution in middle Georgia- Thanks to Hal Povenmire

The terrestrial source for tektites is supported by well-documented evidence. The chemical and isotopic composition of tektites indicates that they are derived from the melting of silica-rich crustal and sedimentary rocks, which are not found on the Moon. In addition, some tektites contain relict mineral inclusions (quartz, zircon, rutile, chromite, and monazite) that are characteristic of terrestrial sediments and crustal and sedimentary source rocks. Also, three of the four tektite strewn fields have been linked by their age and chemical and isotopic composition to known impact craters. A number of different geochemical studies of tektites from the Australasian strewn field concluded that these tektites consist of melted Jurassic sediments or sedimentary rocks that were weathered and deposited about 167 million years ago.

Tektites have dark, glassy like appearance, from the author's collection.

Although it is widely accepted that the formation of and widespread distribution of tektites requires the intense (superheated) melting of near-surface sediments and rocks at the impact site and the following high-velocity ejection of this material from the impact crater, the exact processes involved remain poorly understood. One possible mechanism for the formation of tektites is by the jetting of highly shocked and superheated melt during the initial contact/compression stage of impact crater formation.

Alternatively, various mechanisms involving the dispersal of shock-melted material by an expanding vapor plume, which is created by a hypervelocity impact, have been used to explain the formation of tektites. Any mechanism by which tektites are created must explain chemical data that suggest that parent material from which tektites were created came from near-surface rocks and sediments at an impact site. In addition, the scarcity of known strewn fields relative to the number of identified Impact craters indicate that very unique and rarely met circumstances are required in order for tektites to be created by a meteorite impact. I believe there are many more tektites in middle Georgia, waiting to be found. If you find a tektite, you have something very special!

CHAPTER 18
THE CAVES OF OAKY WOODS AND MIDDLE GEORGIA

Many early pioneers into central Georgia reported discovering limestone caves that went underground to who knows where! Stories of Indian caves and secret passages to Alabama or parts unknown became common in early Georgia History books. Legends of adventurous persons disappearing into the caves and never returning to their families have been told, but proof is sadly lacking! A few of these caves existed in Oaky Woods, but they are more common in South Houston County, extending down into southwest Georgia. Most of the caves in Oaky Woods might have been abandoned water wells which may still exist, so be careful out there!

A few years ago, Stephen Hammock, who was the Robins Air Force Base Archaeologist at the time, and this writer, were requested by an Elko area landowner to investigate some limestone caves on his property. On a hot and damp day, we were shown the caves which started at the surface and meandered in a disjointed fashion down into the earth. The limestone rocks on the surface were carved with various letters and dates which seemed to date from the late 1800's to early 1900's but were mostly hidden by algae and moss.

Stephen Hammack, Former RAFB Archaeologist, explores a cave in south Houston County

Apparently early pioneers were also fascinated by the caves and visited them, perhaps to have picnic lunches and ponder the meanings of the caves. Stephen bravely entered the cave with a flashlight but had only proceeded a short distance when he yelled back to me that the tunnel had grown too narrow to crawl through any further. A few minutes later, he came crawling back out, covered with dirt and spider webs, but glad to have had the adventure. What did we prove?

That these caves do exist in central Georgia, that they were not constructed by man and they are mostly vertical, following the natural flow of water down into the ground. In the early Georgia time period, there were rumors of these limestone caves entered the earth and came out somewhere in Macon County. Supposedly, they were used by Indians to escape white settlers or to hide confederate gold! We could find no basis in fact for these theories, but don't let the truth ruin a great story!

Carvings on a stone wall, next to a cave in Houston County, seem to date from the late 1800's to early 1900s.

The vast majority of the caves we see or hear about are solution caves in limestone. These caves are formed by flowing underground water dissolving the rock material. They are only one feature of what geologists know as karst topography, a land surface characterized by bedrock which has been dissolved by chemical weathering rather than worn away by abrasion. Karst surfaces are commonly marked by sinkholes, caves, and an absence of surface streams. Although karst topography may form on any type of soluble rock, it is most extensively and intensively developed on limestone. Limestone is a sedimentary rock made up of particles deposited in layers at the earth's surface (including under the sea). It may be deposited in several ways, but the particles are always made up of calcium carbonate ($CaCO_3$), usually in the form of piled-up shells and skeletal materials from marine organisms such as oysters, corals, and snails. What is now a thriving coral reef in a tropical ocean will one day be a layer of limestone containing coral fossils.

When bare limestone is exposed at the earth's surface, it is subject to the attack of rainwater weakly acidified by the small amount of carbon dioxide in the atmosphere. However, when rainwater percolates through the soil it absorbs more carbon dioxide, which is formed by the decay of plant material. Thus, if the limestone is soil-covered, the acid attack is much more intense. Climate also plays a role in this solution process.

Now let us look at how flowing water actually hollows out the limestone into caves. When precipitation falls on a porous rock layer, it soaks into the rock (infiltration) and seeps downward under the force of gravity. Most limestone is not porous but is cut by numerous cracks called joints. Water seeps downward along these joints, eventually reaching a level where all fractures and openings are full of water. The upper limit of this water-filled zone is known as the water table. The water beneath the water table flows laterally and drains from the rock at low points, or springs. It is this lateral flow of ground water which forms caves. When water first seeps into the limestone from the soil, it is very rich in carbon dioxide. It dissolves limestone rapidly, losing most, but not all, of its ability to dissolve. This rapid surface solution creates sinkholes and vertical shafts. However, when the descending water reaches the water table it can still dissolve more limestone.

As it moves laterally in a thin zone just below the water table, it enlarges the cracks through which it is flowing. If one crack is somewhat larger, it transmits more water flow. The larger volume of water is capable of dissolving more limestone, so this crack grows faster than the others. As this process perpetuates itself, one crack eventually carries the vast majority of the flow and is enlarged into a cave. The cave, then, is a water conduit. It collects water from one area through sinkholes or cracks in the limestone and transmits it to another area through a naturally formed plumbing network. Most limestone caves form as a result of this water circulation. Their original hydrologic role frequently is obscured by the breakup of the cave into many isolated segments due to roof collapse, sediment buildup, or massive mineral deposition. Indeed, local valleys may deepen until the cave is left high above ground-water level, and totally dry. Where might such conditions and processes take place in Georgia?

Anytime you're around caves or wet areas- watch out for cotton mouth moccasins!

Obviously, in areas where limestone exists. The two general areas of limestone outcrop in Georgia-one in the northwest, the other in the southwest-are made up of very different types of limestone. When water first seeps into the limestone from the soil, it is very rich in carbon dioxide. It dissolves limestone rapidly, losing most, but not all, of its ability to dissolve. This rapid surface solution creates sinkholes and vertical shafts. However, when the descending water reaches the water table it can still dissolve more limestone. As it moves laterally in a thin zone just below the water table, it enlarges the cracks through which it is flowing. If one crack is somewhat larger, it transmits more water flow. The larger volume of water is capable of dissolving more limestone, so this crack grows faster than the others. As this process perpetuates itself, one crack eventually carries the vast majority of the flow and is enlarged into a cave. The cave, then, is a water conduit. It collects water from one area through sinkholes or cracks in the limestone and transmits it to another area through a naturally formed plumbing network. Most limestone caves form as a result of this water circulation. Their original hydrologic role frequently is obscured by the breakup of the cave into many isolated segments due to roof collapse, sediment buildup, or massive mineral deposition. Indeed, local valleys may deepen until the cave is left high above ground-water level, and totally dry. Where might such conditions and processes take place in Georgia? Obviously, in areas where limestone exists.

The limestones in northwestern Georgia are very old-about 350 million years old. They are very hard and dense, and water can only move through them along joints. They frequently are exposed on the slopes of long mountain ridges; therefore, water entering the limestones must sink long distances downward before moving laterally. This area of Georgia contains many caves with deep pits, the result of solution by descending water. In fact, the deepest pit in the United States is in northwestern Georgia: 586 ft. deep, about the height of the tallest Atlanta skyscrapers. It is easy to see why cave exploring in this area must be approached with caution.

In southwestern Georgia the limestones are distinctly different. They are much younger-only 25 million years old-and they are much more porous. In between the pieces of shell and other grains are voids- pore spaces where water may move. This porosity is unusual for limestone. There also are joints which give the water even easier paths to travel. That area of Georgia extending from the southwest corner of the State through Albany to Houston County on the northeast, and characterized by a relatively flat land surface, is known as the Dougherty Plain. In Houston County, these limestone caves are mostly found around Henderson and Grovania. This area is underlain by these limestones. Within the limestones there are sinkholes and cavities.

However, because the limestone is relatively flat and close to the level of the Flint River, which drains the area, most of these are water filled. The sinkholes can be seen on aerial photographs and on topographic maps. We know the caves exist here because water wells have intercepted them, and because large perennial springs in limestone, such as Radium Springs, usually are fed by flow from open conduits. The eastern edge of the Dougherty Plain is marked by a long, low ridge variously known as the Curry Ridge or the Pelham Escarpment. This ridge is the edge of the overlying layers of rock, and here some limestone is exposed at slightly higher elevations. Thus, there are a few caves above the water table. Thanks to Dr Barry Beck, Ph.D., Georgia Southwestern University for his booklet, 'An Introduction to caves and Cave Exploring in Georgia" for some of this information. Caves are just one of the many fascinating natural features that you may encounter in Central Georgia.

CHAPTER 19
THE SAND DUNES OF CENTRAL GEORGIA

When you go south on highway 247 from Kathleen, Georgia, you may have noticed the sand dunes on the side of the road, just before you cross Big Indian creek and before you get to the Houston County landfill. The southern part of Oaky Woods is just past the landfill.

These sand dunes are the result of the last ice age. In Georgia, sand dunes or sandhills can be found in three distinct places: at the seashore, along the fall line, and along the eastern banks of Coastal Plain rivers and streams.

The dunes along riverbanks and streams, like those in Houston County, are also known as riverine sandhills. These dunes, found only on the eastern side of rivers, are believed to have been created by strong winds during the late Pleistocene era 20,000 years ago and formed of deep, coarse, riverine alluvial sand. Most inland aeolian (wind-formed) dunes associated with rivers on the Georgia Coastal Plain probably date to glacial periods. Direct dating of the dune sand shows that dunes formed between 30,000 and 15,000 years ago. But the last ice age lasted about 110,000 years and ended about 12,000 years ago.

Some of the Trussell clan, Jack, left, Ava, Brandon and Analyssa at the sand dunes near Highway 247, south of Kathleen, Ga

Back then the air was very cold and dry as most moisture was tied up in the glaciers. We never had glaciers in Georgia, but they did extend down into Ohio.

The sandhills along the seashore mark current coastlines, while those found along the fall line show where ancient coastlines were. Areas like Crawford and Taylor Counties have deep pockets of sand from what is called the fall line, an ancient sea shore.

Unlike coastal areas and the fall line, riverine sandhills were created over time as strong westerly winds deposited exposed river bottom sand along the eastern shore of certain rivers. The dunes in the Albany area are huge and were formed by erosion of sand from the Flint River and extend over 5 miles along the eastern bank of the Flint. Next time you pass the Houston County sand dunes, appreciate the fact that you're looking at a little bit of ancient history!

The mastodon once walked across Oaky Woods but died out about 12,000 years ago. photo courtesy Royal British Columbia Museum

CHAPTER 20

FISHING IN OAKY WOODS

Fishing is allowed in Oaky Woods anytime the area is open, but the opportunity is very limited to three openings onto the Ocmulgee River where you can bank fish or perhaps work a small kayak or boat into the water. Many years ago, the Land Search Committee for the local State Park /Public Fishing Area that I was on considered damming up Big Grocery Creek to form a large lake. But Weyerhaeuser Company, who owned the land at the time, was not interested in selling it and there was some doubt as to whether the creek had enough water flow to keep a lake filled. Big Grocery Creek can get very low or even dry at times. It starts in the drain near the Larry Ross Campground and has only a few natural springs.

The committee only had a very few good options and we settled on the Andel property that we know today as the Flat Creek Public Fishing area, close to Perry. I think we made a good selection and the PFA is one of the most popular in the state in terms of visitors. I have written several stories about Flat Creek PFA over the years and strongly suggest that you check it out!

But if you want to get away and drop a fishing line in the Ocmulgee River in Oaky Woods and try for bream or a large catfish- go for it! But there are some other good options close by!

Many middle Georgia anglers drive to big reservoirs that are at least an hour's driving time away and pass right by some of the best fishing that is available almost out the back door! In Houston County, two large lakes are connected by Mossy Creek and they are **Houston Lake** and **Lake Joy**. Both are located between the rapidly growing areas of Warner Robins and Perry. Over the years, both lakes have surrendered some huge bass, but they also offer good fishing for crappie, bream and catfish. Lake Joy is located on lake Joy Road, which crosses the dam. Immediately below it lies the headwaters of Houston Lake and both lakes have existed since the mid 1800's. First, let's take a closer look at Houston Lake.

Soon after Houston County was formed in 1821, early settlers dammed up Mossy Creek to set up a grist mill to process corn into flour. The mill grew into a sawmill and textile plant that made cotton and wool cloth. Later the plant made china dishes from the red clay, abundant in the area, and early fishermen would sit around the wood burning stove in the small local store and tell big fish stories. Due to changing economic conditions, the mill eventually went out of business and was dismantled for parts. But the lake remained a local recreation destination and Houston Lake Golf Course was built around it. The lake was private until Tropical storm Alberto blew through in 1994 and dropped 15-20 inches of rain in a short amount of time. The heavy flood that resulted sent a deluge of water over Houston Lake dam and washed it out, along with most other dams in central Georgia.

Because it would cost a huge amount of money to rebuild the dam to modern standards, home owners around the lake and public officials soon came to a compromise whereby the lake dam would be rebuilt with federal funds if the lake became public. Shortly after this decision, the lake dam was constructed, and the Houston County Commissioners worked with the Georgia DNR Fisheries Office in Fort Valley to install a short pier, parking lot and boat ramp. The lake is a huge recreational draw for Houston County.

Fishing has been popular at the lake, but a heavy cover of various aquatic weeds has hindered fishing and boating access in the past. The weed problem has been partially addressed with routine herbicide treatments coordinated and funded by the Houston Lake Alliance, a citizen's group, headed by Jack Nash, interested in the long - term health of the lake. This has been an expensive under taking but the treatments have been effective and today the lake is much more fishable and boat friendly. If you would like to contribute to the Alliance's effort, you can do so by mailing a contribution of any amount to the Perry Area Historical Society, P.O. Box 2174, Perry, 31069. The Alliance now functions as a part of the Perry Historical Society for administrative purposes, says Ellie Loudermilk, Society Director. Make the check payable to: Perry Area Historical Society and write in the memo field: HLA or Houston Lake Alliance.

The rules of the lake are simple. Fishing is allowed daily from dawn to dusk, boats must operate at no wake, idle speed. No Shooting, hunting, alcohol, swimming, or jet skis is allowed, and other Georgia fishing laws apply. There is only one boat ramp, but it is sufficient. Also, Houston County maintains a portable toilet on site

The lake is about 140 acres, but a bridge across the lake from the number 10 golf tee box blocks passage into some of the lake. Anglers are warned to stay back 100 feet from the bridge to avoid being hit by a golf ball!

Houston Lake is fairly shallow with some 8-10-foot water out from the dam and much of the lake is only 3-6 feet deep. Local angler Michael Lynn lives close to the lake and fishes it on a frequent basis with great results. He honed his fishing teeth on the Military Bass Anglers Fishing Trail and won the 1988 national tournament on Lake Kerr in North Carolina. The grand prize was a nice Ranger Boat with Yamaha Motor and Michael and I fished from it on March 31, 2018. For a 30-year-old boat, it performed great and we managed to put several fish in the boat on a very slow day. Michael is a catch and release angler in 2017 he caught his biggest bass, a 9.5 pounder, from Houston Lake. It hit a Strike King jerk bait, in ghost color, only about 50 yards north of the boat ramp!

He likes to fish open water and normally confines himself to the lower 1/3 of the lake that is mostly weed free. We fished in the late morning and could only draw interest from chain pickerel and yellow perch that hit chrome jerk baits. Michael likes to make long casts and then slowly twitch the baits to draw a predatory strike reaction from a bass. Some of his favorite locations are the north east corner of the lake, out from the Houston Lake Clubhouse, where there is a lot of submerged old stumps. He also likes to hit around the shoreline structure out from the number 10 golf green, then tries the sea wall out from number 11. He sometimes works this area with a June bug or pumpkin seed worm around the weeds but prefers the open water just out from the cover.

According to Brandon Baker, Georgia DNR Fisheries Biologist from Fort Valley, Houston Lake offers some good fishing and the Georgia DNR has yearly stockings of catfish, totaling 16,000, since 2014. They also stocked 60 bass in the lake in 2017 in the two to six-pound size, and some threadfin shad to increase the feed available to the bass. He says the bream and crappie fishing is good around docks and the deep- water stump fields. Now let's look at Lake Joy.

Also starting as an early pioneer grist mill, the area was known as Tharpe's Mill Pond, then changed later to Lake Joy. The main lake is owned by Wilbur Long and managed by Taylor Long. Taylor says the main lake is 90 acres. Home owners around the lake own property down to the water line. Fishing and boating access is 5.00 per day from dawn to dusk, bank fishing is 3.00, but the bank fishing area is small. There is a small white, pay lock box at the boat ramp. The rules are the same as Houston Lake.

James Fletcher with nice Lake Joy bass

    James Fletcher is a lake resident and retired Robins Air Force Base civil service. He has fished the lake for many years from a small Jon boat, powered by a paddle and his best fishing pal is John Allison. He and I have fished together several times in recent months with good results. James is a stealth fisherman and says the shallow water requires that anglers move around quietly to avoid spooking the fish. He prefers to fish the back of the lake where it is weedy, but with less fishing pressure. He often catches good bass in water that is only 1-3 feet deep. His best bass from 1986, weighed 12 pounds, 6 ounces and hit a Johnson silver minnow, dressed with a pork rind. His next best is a 11 pounder that hit a crappie minnow in January 2014 in the main lake channel. He is a catch and release angler, but these two whoppers are hanging on his wall!

Lake Joy is densely weeded and by summertime only the deep channel areas are free of weeds. James sneaks around from open pocket to pocket of water and drops in an unweighted June bug worm and lets it sink to the bottom. He then begins a very slow retrieve where he lets the swimming action of the lure draw a strike. Most bass will be in the 1 to 2 pound class, with a few chain pickerel and mud fish thrown in. James likes to bream fish on the small sandy bottom areas around the shore line and around boat docks. For crappie, he often uses live minnows in the open channels.

Although Lake Joy is said to be the "Home of the Big One that got away", local fishing legend Randy Zell has put some whoppers in the boat. His parents lived on the lake and he fished it often. In the early 1990's he caught a bass that weighed 15 pounds, 7 ounces and says that he has caught 20 bass that weighted over 10 pounds from lake Joy. Some of his big bass are hanging on the wall at Chucks Gun and Pawn in Warner Robins. He recalls another bass caught by another angler that he saw that weighed 17 pounds, so the opportunity is there to pull in a trophy bass. He says the lake is loaded with dark colored crayfish, so he uses a black grape plastic lizard to match the bass food.

Like James Fletcher, he says bass won't chase bait far in the weeds, so he drops the bait in every open hole in the grass and swims it slowly. The lake is also loaded with frog and tadpoles, so a black floating frog will produce bass. For big bream, he recommends the back, south side of the lake and suggests Louisiana pinks fished on the bottom with no cork. Try these two home grown lakes soon!

Also Close to Oaky Woods are White Water Park and the Mennonite Pond in Macon County. Sometimes you just want to get away to a quite retreat, loose the crowds and see some different water! In central Georgia, two local large ponds in Macon County deserve a date on your outdoor calendar for great fishing and outdoor fun. First, we will take a close look at White Water Creek Park, owned and operated by Macon County. The park has a long history in Macon County and it started as a pioneer grist mill for early settlers when the county was formed in 1837. Georgia Power build a hydro power generator on the site back in the 1940's but it was later abandoned, and the land became a state park for many years. Several years ago, the State gave up management of some of it smaller parks and Macon County assumed ownership of the Park. Today, Regina McDuffie is county manager, Armard Burnett is Recreation Director and the White-Water Park Manager is Darin Barfield. The park is 482 acres, the lake itself about 65 acres, as measured on Google Earth. The lake stretches from just above the campground eastward to the dam. You can access many more hundreds of acres of water upstream.

Darin Barfield, manager of White-Water Park, with a nice bluegill.

Recently Darin Barfield and I unloaded his small 10- foot boat at the park boat ramp and headed up stream to try to put some bream into the boat. The middle section of the lake has plenty of hydrilla, but Barfield keeps a boat channel open so that anglers can get to the main channel. In the upstream section, it is hard to miss the main channel of White Water Creek as it is well defined and has a steady current. If you like good stream fishing, this could be your honey hole as the stream is fishable 2.5 miles upstream. There are many small pockets of grass and marsh to explore, just off from the channel.

Barfield and I dangled crickets under a cork to every fishy spot as we slowly drifted downstream. The bream and bass usual hangout along the edges of the grass in the calmer water and we had steady interest in our offerings. We put numerous bream in the boat, everything from three fingers in size to one pound plus bluegills. Barfield says the south side of the lake usually produces more bream. Straight out from the boat ramp, about 100 yards, is some open water that has a lot of debris scattered on the bottom and this is a bream hangout, says Barfield. Look for the wood fence on the south bank and fish about 50 yards north of it, in the large open pockets of water. The best crappie location is the deeper water out in front of the dam but drifting a minnow down the creek will pay off too. Geno Reeves is a regular bass angler in the lake and recently he has pulled in two whopper bass, one 10.4 pounds and another 11.2 pounds. Both these bass were caught in June on in the deeper water just out from the swimming beach on June bug colored worms. Don't be surprised by a large jack fish, black fish or catfish as there are plenty in the lake. Kayak anglers can put in behind the dam, next to White Water Baptist Church, and fish downstream. Duck hunters sometimes pay their five dollars, put in at the lake boat ramp, and shoot ducks in the upstream section.

Rob Weller, DNR Fisheries Biologist, Albany office, says White Water lake is a popular local pond but the high amount of water that passes over the dam can make it difficult to manage, but it still can provide good fishing. The "Bragging Board" in the office, managed by Janet Mendez, has numerous pictures of large bass in the 8-12-pound range posted on it and the largest known bass from the lake weighed 13 pounds. Whitewater Creek Park is open year-round, and offers excellent tent and rv camping, pavilions, fishing, hiking and cabin rental. For the kids, there is a small fishing pond, playground equipment, a sand beach and a splash pad.

A few years ago, Macon County used local Splost monies and a state grant to upgrade the Park facilities, so you will find the park in great condition. The park is open from 7 a.m. until 10 p.m. and the office is open from 8 a.m. until 5 p.m. Park admission for fishing is 5.00 per day, per vehicle and you can pay at the office or the pay box at the boat ramp. For more information, go www.maconcountyga.gov/whitewater-creek-park.cfm or call 478-472-8171 or cell 478-244-2475. The Park is located at 165 White Water Road, Oglethorpe, Georgia.

MENNONITE POND

Also, in Macon County is the "Mennonite Pond", but it's no longer owned by the Mennonites, a sect of the Amish. In 1986, Dave McKay, a retired teacher and coach from Ohio, moved to Macon County and purchased 300 acres which included the pond, but the name has stuck to it. On Google earth, the pond is named Horse Head Creek lake, just in case you look it up. McKay leases the majority of his land to Barrington and Highbrighton Dairies, which has 7,500 cows in the county. There is a large Mennonite population in the area that moved here in 1956 from Virginia. They are a positive, hard-working group and are a big part of the local farming and business community. They accept some conveniences of modern life, like cars and electricity, but reject movies and TV. The Mennonites allowed fishing for a low, three dollars per day fee and McKay has continued that practice. The White House Farm Bed and Breakfast and the Deitsch Haus restaurant, both operated by the Yoder family in Montezuma, offer visitors a glimpse of life in a

Mennonite community. Give them a try after you put some fish in the cooler!

Recently I had the chance to talk Chuck Williams, the owner of Chucks Gun and Pawn in Warner Robins and asked him where in middle Georgia are fishermen going fishing? Chuck was a former real estate agent who purchased Chuck's Bait and Tackle from former owner Chuck Lawson many years ago. Today the expanded business at **603 Watson Blvd** is one of the state's top outdoor businesses for anything related to fishing and hunting. They have new and used guns, archery equipment and a bow -tech on staff. He also carries live bait, including minnows. Chuck said that a lot of anglers go to Macon County to the Mennonite Pond, which offers great bream and bass fishing. So, with that information, I loaded up the boat and headed south. My fishing partner of this trip was Judge George Nunn of Perry. Now in semi- retired status as a senior Judge, he served many years as Chief Judge of the Houston Judicial Circuit. It was my honor to serve that court as Chief Probation Officer for many years. Now Judge Nunn and I do important things like fish!

Judge George Nunn of Perry caught this nice bream from the Mennonite pond in Macon County on a cricket.

To reach the Mennonite pond, take highway 224 from Perry and turn left onto Mennonite Church Road. Travel 1.7 mile to a sharp left curve in the road. This curve will be about 200 yards past the Mid

Georgia Farm Service store. At the curve, turn right on Duck pond road. Travel this road for a short 300 yards and take a left on an unnamed, small dirt road. Travel 1.3 miles to the farm house and small wooded building on the left where you pay your $3.00 per person to fish. Follow the road down to the pond and the boat ramps.

When you pull into the house area, look for the pay box next to the old wooden building, usually sitting on the ground next to the door. Take an envelope from the box, put your money in it and write your tag number on the envelope, then deposit it in the slot in the door. The 80-acre pond allows 15 crappie and 25 bream to be kept each day, but all bass fishing is catch and release and there are some whoppers in the lake. There are two boat ramps, one on the west side of the dam and the other next to the irrigation pipes/ switches on the west bank, near the middle of the pond. Fishing is allowed daily from sunrise to dusk, no night fishing allowed.

Judge Nunn and I fished for bass around the shoreline cover with Texas rigged worms and surface minnow baits, but the bass were elusive. Usually the bass hang around the debris in the back of the pond but a weather front had passed through the night before and the bass had lockjaw! A floating frog, chrome rapala or yellow white spinner bait is the usually the ticket in these areas. We also used worms and crickets in the backs of coves and around overhanging brushes to put a lot of bluegills and shellcrackers in the boat. We ran across a few other anglers and they had caught lots of bream, pulled in from just off the grass edges. We confirmed that the Mennonite pond is a great place to fish!

CHAPTER 21
A CHAMPION TREE GROWS IN BONAIRE

My Father, Grady Rufus Trussell, planted three sawtooth oak trees on his property on Feagin Mill Road in 1964. Recently one of them became a Georgia Champion Tree for being the largest in the state. A champion tree is the largest known tree of a particular species, according to the Georgia Champion Tree Program's website. Angela Woolen wrote a story about the tree a few years ago in the Macon Telegraph, entitled, "Bonaire Tree Recognized as Largest of its Kind". The sawtooth oak tree, measuring 95 feet high with a 126-inch circumference, is still doing well and hopefully will continue to live many years into the future.

I was researching tree certifications while at Oaky Woods and realized I might have a champion tree on the family property. The state-listed champion listed on the Georgia Forestry web site didn't appear to be as large as the one we had in our yard, so I started to investigate the nomination process.

From left, Grady Trussell, Jr, Peggy Lobertini, John Trussell and Joe Trussell pose by the State Champion Sawtooth Oak tree, on Feagin Mill Road in Houston County

It took about six months for the paperwork and measuring of the tree to prove that the Trussell's had a winning tree. The champion tree in Bonaire, near the corner of Cartwright Road and Feagin Mill Road, has been cared for by the family for nearly 50 years, but a new family lives there now. Sawtooth oaks are not native to the U.S. but are fast-growing trees that produce nuts in about seven to eight years and they produce many hundreds of pounds every year once they are mature. This makes them ideal for wildlife enthusiasts and hunters who plant the trees to attract deer, wild hogs and squirrel. The oaks were distributed by the Georgia Forestry Commission in the 1960s as year-old seedlings and they still sell young trees on their website.

This tree is fairly young in age to be a champion, but I attribute the success of the champion tree to having enough nutrients its entire life, due to the septic system near its roots and we added fertilizer to the roots. Had the tree been out in the woods, dealing with lack of rain and shade from other trees, it probably would not have grown nearly as big

Do you have a champion tree on your land or know of a huge tree somewhere? The next chapter discusses how to get a tree certified.

CHAPTER 22

DO YOU HAVE A CHAMPION TREE ON YOUR PROPERTY?

It is no secret that we think trees are pretty special! We plant them, and we carefully watch them grow, then we study them from many different angles. At harvest time they provide a vast multitude of products for our homes and businesses and the monies earned from trees puts food on our tables. If you think about trees too much, you can get sentimental about them, but that can be a good thing. Joyce Kilmer, (1886- 1918) a lover of nature, and poet, died a hero in WW1, is mainly known for the poem "TREES".

    I THINK that I shall never see
    A poem lovely as a tree.

    A tree whose hungry mouth is prest
    Against the sweet earth's flowing breast;

    A tree that looks at God all day,   5
    And lifts her leafy arms to pray;

    A tree that may in summer wear
    A nest of robins in her hair;

    Upon whose bosom snow has lain;
    Who intimately lives with rain.   10

    Poems are made by fools like me,
    But only God can make a tree.

Kilmer wrote a great poem, but he was also very practical and kept a big woodpile next to his house to stoke the fireplace and keep the winter chill at bay. Perhaps he thought of trees in a sentimental way, but also knew that wood was a very useful product. Another way to think about trees is to celebrate the biggest and best among the species of trees. Perhaps it's an American thing, but we love to see how tall a tree can grow, and we like to keep records of our best trees. That was the idea behind the state and national champion tree registry that has been maintained since 1940 by American Forests, a non-profit conservation organization. In the September 1940 issue of AMERICAN FORESTS magazine, concerned forester Joseph Sterns published his article "Let's Find and Save the Biggest Trees." Sterns wasn't referring to the famous and historic trees that were already protected, but the giants left standing in virgin forests.

Forester Danny Hamsley inspects the Swamp Chestnut Oak State Co- Champion tree in Oaky Woods

Since that call to locate and measure the largest trees of each species, American Forests has maintained the NATIONAL REGISTER OF BIG TREES, a list of the biggest trees in America. The Big Tree Program is active in all 50 states and the District of Columbia and is used as a model for several Big Tree programs around the world. With sponsorship from the Davey Expert Tree Company, since 1989, the National Big Tree Program has been able to reach a wider audience and promote the same message for over 70 years: regardless of size, all trees are champions of the environment.

To be eligible, a species must be recognized as native or naturalized in the continental United States, as documented in Elbert L. Little Jr.'s *Checklist of United States Trees (Native and Naturalized)*, published in 1979 as *Agricultural Handbook 541* by the United States Department of Agriculture. At present 747 native and 79 naturalized trees are eligible, for a total of 826 eligible species and varieties.

American Forests uses the following formula to calculate a point score for each tree so that they may be compared to others: Trunk Circumference (in inches) + Height (in feet) + Average Crown Spread (in feet) = Total Points

The current list of National Champion Trees is available online. In addition to the national list, several states, counties, and cities maintain their own list of local Champion Trees. Many are on public ground and can be visited without obtaining prior permission. The public may nominate trees as well.

As of this year, the largest National Champion Tree is a giant sequoia in California. Known as the General Sherman tree, it is some 83.8 m (274.9 feet) tall, 31.1 m (1,024 inches) in circumference and 32.5 m (106.5 feet) in average crown spread. Now let's talk Georgia trees.

Do you have a Georgia or National tree champion on your property? Perhaps that giant hickory or red cedar that you have been looking at since you were a child may qualify, so check it out! The Georgia Forestry Commission oversees the Champion Tree Program in Georgia and the state coordinator is Scott Griffin. For a tree to be considered it must meet all of the following criteria.

1. The tree must have an erect woody perennial stem, or trunk, at least 9.5 inches in circumference measured 4.5 feet from the ground, with a definitely formed crown of foliage, and is at least 13 feet in total height.

2. To be eligible for the Georgia Champion Tree Program, a species must be recognized as native or naturalized in the continental United States. There are species currently on Georgia's Champion Tree list not listed in the Handbook because in the past any tree species was accepted. The goal is to remove these species over time as these champions cease to exist. Any naturalized tree species considered invasive will not be considered. A complete list of Georgia invasive trees can be viewed at Gainvasives.org.

Georgia Champion Tree Program - How to Score a Tree

Three measurements - trunk circumference, tree height, average crown spread - need to be submitted on the Georgia Champion Tree nomination form. Instructions on how to obtain these measurements are listed below. Use the following calculations to get an estimated total score of your tree. Punch in the numbers into the online form and it will do the final tally for you at www. gfc.state.ga.us /forestmanagement /championtree.cfm. A tree that scores within 5% of a champion will be recognized as a Georgia Co-Champion.

1. **Trunk circumference is measured in inches.** The trunk circumference is the distance around the tree. It is measured 4.5 feet above the ground level.

2. **Tree height is measured in feet.** Tree height is accurately measured using a clinometer, laser, hypsonometer, or other specialized tools. If these tools are not available, height can be estimated using the Boy Scout "stick method

3. The average crown is measured in feet. This is the dip line from the end of the branches

CHAPTER 23

OAKY WOODS FIRE TOWER FADES INTO HISTORY

It stands like a mighty sentinel against the bright, beautiful blue sky of Oaky Woods. The 110 feet of cold steel is a lonely reminder of the things that used to be.

Since the late 1980s, the state has steadily cut its fire tower staff in favor of what officials describe as less costly and more effective forestry air patrols to spot forest fires. The man on top of the tower has been replaced with the man in a Cessna plane. As a result, part of Georgia's history is slowly disappearing, almost without notice. Many years ago, a State Forest Ranger would climb the tower during the dry fire season, usually in late summer and look for whiffs of smoke on the horizon. Once a suspicious spot of smoke was spotted, he would radio headquarters and a fire crew would drive to check it out. The goal was to spot a small forest fire and put it out before it became a major fire. The Oaky Woods tower has been unused for many years and was vandalized about 10 years ago and some of the windows were broken out, but the structure is still very strong. The tower is now posted against trespassers and no public access is allowed. Despite being largely abandoned, it's a historically significant icon that I hope will stand for many years.

Information from the Georgia Forestry Commission reveals a quite transition over time. The large majority, 137 of the state's 144 still-existing towers, are no longer staffed. Of those, 119 are listed as "antenna towers", and this does include the Oaky Woods tower, so it's is still useful. Most towers sit empty most of the time, although forestry commission employees climb up occasionally during fire season - usually whenever bad weather keeps air patrols grounded.

Most towers in the state's southern section are steel-frame and manufactured by the Aermotor Corp. of Chicago - a company best known for making the windmills that dotted the landscape in an earlier era. Like the once-common windmills, fire towers are fading. There used to be a fire tower on Fire Tower Road in South Houston County. Today the tower is gone, and no one seems to know what happened to it. I made several inquiries to the Forestry Commission about its fate, but never got a reply. I have to assume it was sold for scrap metal. Today all we have is the road name, Fire Tower Road, but no fire tower! But we still have the Oaky Woods tower and I hope it is left alone!

Human visitors to the top of the Oaky Woods tower are rare. In their absence, forest critters have adapted to the tower. Buzzards like to visit and roost on the cross bars, and flying squirrels sometimes nest in the cab. Owls also swoop in from time to time and there is always a steady flight of wasps around the tower. Visitors get to gaze at the mighty steel frame that has endured countless lightning strikes, violent winds and thousands of inches of rain. I was able to climb the tower many years ago, with permission, and share the great view with Neil Herring, Public Relations spokesman for the National Sierra Club.

the author sits at the top of the fire tower, admiring the great view..

Herring produced a short interview/video tape that aired to Sierra Club members and the press in our effort to preserve Oaky Woods. From the top of the tower, the beautiful green canopy of trees stretches across the horizon like it never ends! As far as the eye could see, there was not a single house in sight.

No, you can't see seven states from the top of the tower, but you can see seven counties! Today, most visitors drive by the fire tower and hardly notice it, but it's a beacon of getting things done the old-fashioned way and a reminder that we must always strive to improve. I have been gazing upon the fire tower for more than 50 years and think it's pretty special. Long may the old fire tower stand!

To preserve the tower, I have nominated it to the list of "Historical Fire Towers" with the Forest Fire Lookout Association and submitted the form and photo to them for the record book. This was done in June 2018. I am hopeful that the damage to the top cab of the tower will be repaired in the future.

Thanks to the Georgia Forestry Commission and Frank Sorrells, Chief of Fire Protection, for their help with the Fire Tower.

CHAPTER 24

GOPHER TORTOISES ROAM OAKY WOODS

There are not many tortoises in Oaky Woods, but I have seen a few over the years, primarily south of Kovac road where the terrain is sandy. They are more common in the sandy soil of Taylor County and South Georgia.

A few years ago, I saw a mature gopher tortoise crossing Watson Blvd, near highway 41, and you probably know that's a busy location. The tortoise made it to the grassy median and I doubted it would survive the balance of the journey. So I stopped, picked up the tortoise and took it to my home until I could get it to a large tract of suitable land a few days later. A few months later I discovered a baby tortoise in my one-acre yard. Had the other tortoise laid an egg that hatched in my yard? Don't know about that, but the baby stayed in my yard on its own free will for two years until it wandered off.

They are now considered threatened across much of their habitat and the Georgia DNR now considers it a priority species for management. The official state reptile of Georgia, the gopher tortoise is a relatively large terrestrial turtle, obtaining a maximum carapace length of 38 cm (15 inches), though averaging 23-28 cm (9-11 inches). Perhaps the most characteristic features of gopher tortoises are the elephantine hind limbs and the flattened, shovel-like forelimbs. It's a reclusive reptile, but if you're in the outdoors a lot, you may occasionally see one crossing a dirt road. Along with sandy soil for burrowing, sunlight availability and abundant herbaceous vegetation are the key habitat requirements for this reptile. Gopher tortoises are a characteristic species of the rapidly disappearing longleaf pine and wiregrass community, which includes sandhills, dry flatwoods, and turkey oak scrub. Historically, this community was represented by an open-canopied forest that allowed abundant sunlight penetration and conditions favorable for a rich growth of herbaceous vegetation. Unfortunately, very little of this naturally occurring habitat still exists; therefore, many tortoises have been forced into artificial habitats, such as roadsides and old fields, that retain the three key requirements. A wide variety of succulent grasses and forbs; fruits, such as those of legumes, are eaten in season. Carrion is occasionally taken.

This gopher tortoise was found near the Houston County line next to his den.

Gopher tortoises dig unbranched burrows up to, and sometimes greater than, 10 m (33 feet) long. The burrows are excavated wide enough to allow room for the tortoise to turn around at any point and may have an enlarged terminal chamber. A single tortoise may dig more than one burrow each season, and occupancy of a burrow by more than one tortoise may occur, at least temporarily.

The gopher tortoise has been termed a "keystone species" of the longleaf pine community, meaning its existence is critical to the existence of many other species. Courtship and mating occur from April through early June. Nesting reaches a peak in early June but may last until mid-July. Females, which may not attain sexual maturity until 19-20 years of age, produce only once clutch each year and usually construct nests in the burrow mounds. An average of six white, nearly spherical eggs are deposited, and hatching follows an incubation period of 97-106 days. Nests and hatchlings are preyed upon by a variety of mammals and snakes, though raccoons are apparently the chief predators at most sites.

The loss and alteration of the longleaf pine-wiregrass community through agricultural and silvicultural activities, urban sprawl, and fire suppression has eliminated many populations and isolated most others. It has been estimated that the average female gopher tortoise in Georgia has an effective rate of reproduction of about 5.8 hatchlings per 10 years, assuming annual egg laying. This naturally low reproduction is only worsened by isolation, unnaturally high populations of certain predators, suboptimal habitat conditions, and other factors. Tortoises forced into roadside habitats due to a lack of suitable surrounding land are obviously more vulnerable to vehicle impacts and collection by humans.

In the old days rattle snake hunters may have unintentionally killed some tortoises. The introduction of gasoline into the burrows of gopher tortoises ("gassing") is a technique used by some rattlesnake hunters to force the snakes to the surface. This practice is typically fatal to all burrow inhabitants and it highly discouraged! Most folks have stopped this practice. In recent years the Georgia DNR has been acquiring tortoise habitat lands in an effort to bring this important species back to healthy numbers and you may see one in Oaky Woods. They can live more than a hundred years and we need to help them survive in central Georgia.

CHAPTER 25

STATE PURCHASES A MAJOR PORTION OF OAKY WOODS

By Author, Georgia Outdoor News 3/23/2011

In 2007 where I and a small group of Oaky Woods supporters started "Save Oaky Woods", we were not given much of a chance of preserving the property, but we just had to try to save middle Georgia's last best wilderness area, and we had to hope that circumstances would change for the better. In December 2010, time was running out when the state made a strong push to purchase a major portion of Oaky Woods and high- level negotiations were taking place. In fact, during the last deer hunt of the year, some of the DNR board members were given a tour of Oaky Woods on Friday December 3 by DNR Asst Commissioner for Operations, Todd Holbrook, and Lauren Curry, DNR Director of Communications. To support the purchase, several members of the "Save Oaky Woods" conservation group, including this writer and Billie Trussell, Alex and Pat Morrow and Art Christie, were present to greet the Board members and offer light refreshments during their visit. The board members seemed very interested in learning more about the property and carefully weighed all the facts related to the possible purchase. On Dec 7, the Land acquisition sub- committee voted 8 to 1 to recommend the purchase to the full board, and then on Dec 8 the full board voted to buy Oaky Woods on a vote of 11-6. The final hurdle was the review of the State Properties Commission. On Monday, Dec 13, they unanimously approved spending $28.7 million in state bond money on 10,015 acres of Oaky Woods and the deal closed out at the end of December. So finally, after many years of speculation and doubt, outdoorsmen saw a rare victory of conservation over development and now a major portion of Oaky Woods will be preserved for all Georgians forever!

Some Natural Resources Board members said the price was too high at $2,874 per acre, but that price fell between two appraisals, thus can be considered a fair market price and the state can only pay appraised value for property. In comparison, Oaky Woods Properties bought it for about $1,600 an acre in 2004 when Weyerhaeuser sold most their Georgia lands, a total of 400,000 acres. With such a large sale, Weyerhaeuser sold the land at depressed prices and many of the new owners resold their lands at a quick profit. The state passed on a chance to buy the Oaky Woods land then and the developers, Charles Ayer, Scott Free, Charlie McGlamery and A. L. Williams, set about to plan for up to 35,000 homes and businesses on the Oaky Woods property, but continued to lease the WMA land to the state. They bought additional entrance right of way, applied for a bridge permit, petitioned Houston County for a waste treatment plant off Kovac Road, and paid for conservation and use assessments. However, when the economy tanked and development plans stalled, the owners and the state started new discussions and thankfully, those discussions where successful. The state was able to purchase the heart of Oaky Woods, with perhaps the most important bear habitat that lies along Big and Little grocery creeks. Also purchased were a 50- foot buffer around the perimeter road, plus the check station, workshop areas and additional river lands.

Georgia DNR Botanist Tom Patrick points out some rare Liverwort plants in Oaky Woods. Right behind him is Wayne Chapman

"Since 2003, the state has conserved over 200,000 acres through purchases, donations and easements," Bert Brantley, a spokesman for Gov. Sonny Perdue, said in a prepared statement after the Natural Resources Board's vote. "The conservation of Oaky Woods is a terrific addition to the state's portfolio." Todd Holbrook, DNR Assistant Commissioner for Operations, said the purchase of Oaky Woods is" a crown jewel of land acquisitions for the DNR and the state has long sought to preserve the property. It is very important to preserve the Oaky Woods habitat for that small, isolated black bear population, the very rare black prairie chalk lands and the many rare plants, flowers and diverse habitat". Kevin Kramer, Chief Region Biologist for DNR's Fort Valley office, said immediate plans for Oaky woods call for the development of a 50- year management plan that will stress habitat improvement for wildlife, increased care of black prairie areas and improved public access. The good stand of pine trees will be managed primarily for wildlife and second for timber production. Currently valued at about 1000 per acre, the trees will provide a long- term cash crop for state revenue. Kramer said that in the past the land was primarily managed for timber production and the state was very limited as to what it could do, because the land was only leased, not owned by the state. Now that the land is state owned, wildlife management will take a front row seat, says Kramer, good news for sportsmen. Raye Jones, long time Oaky Woods WMA manager says that although he is disappointed that the state could not buy the whole WMA, he is very pleased that a major portion of the WMA will be preserved forever and looks forward to improved wildlife management opportunities on the WMA.

Presently, Oaky Woods WMA is comprised of 19, 401 acres and of that amount, 16,286 is leased from Oaky Woods LLC. With the states purchase of 10,015 acres and 1117 acres already owned by the state along the Ocmulgee River, Oaky Woods will have 11,132 acres of state owned land. In addition, Houston County now includes 1998 acres in the WMA, located on the south end of the property, around the land fill, thus the total acres that includes state and county land is 13,130 acres, thus Oaky Woods will retain two –thirds of its land mass, a pretty good outcome, says Kramer. In the initial WMA contract, the state was set to purchase 9,595 acres, but in final negotiations, the owners offered an additional 420 acres on the south end of the proposed land map, which brought the total land purchased to 10,015 acres. The attached map does NOT include the 420 acres because the property lines were being drawn at press time. But basically, the 420 acres extends in a narrow band from the south end of this map and continues in a south direction to the mouth of Big Indian Creek at the Ocmulgee River. This is cut over, flood plain land, but as Kramer said, the trees will grow back, and this is an important addition. The big question now is whether the state will be able to maintain the privately-owned land in the lease, primarily the west and south portions of the WMA, and keep it in the WMA. Both Holbrook and Kramer said that decision depends on the new state budget and last year the DNR saw significant cuts in its lease funds and about 4,500 acres of Ocmulgee WMA, lands north of highway 96, that were cut from that WMA. Seventy five percent of lease monies tickle down from the federal government and the state only contributed 25%, but state law makers cut that 25%. Hopefully, those cuts can be avoided in 2011, and now is a good time to discuss this issue with your local Representatives. On Oaky Woods, the lease is 12.50 per acre, the costliest in the state and Ayers says the tax runs 11.25 per acre because the owners cannot take advantage of conservation tax cuts due to their eventual plans to develop some of the property.

On the December 1-4 deer hunt, wildlife Biologist Bobby Bonds says that 448 hunters checked in and took 108 deer, 66 bucks and 42 does and that works out to a success ratio of 25%, pretty good for a WMA hunt. The rut runs into late November and the first of December on Oaky Woods, so this hunt catches the tail end of the rut and some hunters reported chasing activity. Mike Taggard of Acworth, Clyde Yoder of Montezuma, Victor Williams and Allen Davis from Snellville, all brought in nice bucks to the check station. Kramer says the deer population is down slightly from the 1980's when it was in the 28 per square mile range, but he now estimates that the population is around 20 per square mile. He says that natural mortality, degraded habitat and food competition caused by wild pigs are primary limiting factors, followed by a very small degree of predation by bears and coyotes during the fawn drop period. But in the near future, the DNR will be planting more native plants and creating more natural openings to increase browse for deer, which should help increase the population. Also, the very limited doe hunting on the WMA is an effort to increase the herd and the population is now below the carrying capacity of the land, says Kramer, so there is room for growth. The last deer hunt of the year, a buck only, sign- in hunt, was held for Jan 1-7, 2011 and now the small game season is underway but check the regs for full details.

Wild pig hunting continues to be a strong draw of interest to hunters at Oaky Woods, but on the Dec 1-4 hunt, only two wild pigs were checked out. Most hunters reported seeing little hog sign which is indicative of a lower wild hog population. Bobby Bond said this probably shows that the wild hogs have been hammered by the small game hunters and predation permit holders during the off season, which is a good thing as wild pigs compete for common deer and turkey food sources. This writer saw several pigs running through the thick cutover areas but could not get a shot at them during the Dec 1-4 hunt. So if you try pig hunting during the small game dates, try the thickest cover you can find. Also try the creek bottoms, thick with maiden cane, along Big Grocery Creek and the slews along the Ocmulgee River. Make sure you take a GPS or compass to avoid getting lost, because when the sun starts to set, it can get spooky down there.

As a side note, middle Georgia hunters and target shooters need to know that the Ocmulgee WMA gun range is now has paid range officers on site to reduce accidents and assist shooters, according to Kramer, and there is still no charge to use the range. Range hours are 10 am to 6pm Tuesday –Saturday and 1pm -6pm on Sunday. The range is closed on Monday and check the DNR website for driving instructions.

In closing, this writer wishes to thank the many individuals and groups who assisted in the long effort to preserve Oaky Woods. Terry Todd at GOA and Steve Burch at GON have been very helpful in bringing breaking news on Oaky Woods to outdoorsmen. Pierre Howard, President of the Georgia Conservancy and Will Wingate, legislative coordinator, toured Oaky Woods with this writer and wrote supportive letters to the DNR Board. At the Georgia Wildlife Federation, Jerry McCollum Glen Dowling, and Sam Stowe provided booth space to the Save Oaky Woods group at their trade shows to talk with effected sportsmen. Thanks to Heather Duncan, and other writers at the Macon telegraph, who wrote several positive stories about Oaky Woods. The Save Oaky Woods Board was also very supportive, especially Sec / Treasurer Alex Morrow, Walt Wood and Art Christie. The Houston County Board of Commissioners, especially outgoing chairman Ned Sanders and incoming Chairman Tommy Stalnaker have been very supportive, as have state employees Todd Holbrook, Steve Freidman, Kevin Kramer, Bobby Bond, Raye Jones and the DNR Board. Principal owner spokesman Charles Ayer always maintained open lines of communication which was greatly appreciated. Brandon Trussell (digitalpeach.com) developed and maintained the Save Oaky Woods web site, a tremendously valuable service. Lastly, thanks to Gov Sonny Perdue, State Senator Ross Tolleson and Oaky Woods LLC for their efforts to preserve Oaky Woods. We will keep the web site active (www.saveoakywoods.com) as we try to inform and educate Georgians to the tremendous value of Oaky woods and look for new opportunities to expand its borders. I hope to see you down at Oaky Woods soon!

CHAPTER 26
STORY BEHIND AMAZING 1862 BEECH CARVING

Tom Jarrell couldn't do much with a pencil and a piece of paper. The fact of the matter was that Tom's writing skills were sadly lacking. But that state of affairs wasn't unusual for a 12-year-old youth on a Southern plantation in 1862. Tom's dad, a farmer, had joined the southern war effort long ago along with all the other able-bodied men, thus nothing but young boys and old men were left to run the farms. Tom had learned that it didn't take much education to pick cotton from dawn to dusk. Just good health and a strong back was all that was required.

John Trussell found this old 1862 carving in a beech tree on Piedmont Refuge in Jones County

Although Tom didn't know much of what was going on in the world, his mamma often talked about the terrible Civil War. He knew that his father had fought in some important battles and had been wounded in the Battle of Shiloh but had miraculously survived. Tom did not understand the reasons for the war, but he did know that he missed his dad and felt abandoned. With so much work to do, social interaction was limited except for church on Sunday and he had little contact with other boys his age. He was lonely and confused. So, he reached out to the only other person who could understand his predicament and that was Willie Jarrell, same age as Tom. Willie was legally a slave on the farm and shared the family name, but unofficially he was Tom's best friend and confidant. The dire conditions of the civil war had forged a strong bond between them for mutual survival.

Willie was basically an unknowing and uninvolved bystander in a struggle that would decide his ultimate fate. He did understand that these were not happy times and that much of his owner's heart, soul and purse was being consumed by the war effort. Most significantly for

Willie, his father was rarely around anymore, as he was rented out to another nearby plantation to earn badly needed extra income for the plantation.

One hot summer evening in 1862, after Tom and Willie had finished their day's labor and polished off a supper of peas, cornbread and fatback, they decided to ramble down to the creek bank. The cool air was settling, and the fireflies were coming out. The fireflies hovered in the low brushes like little fairies and gave the evening an almost magical feeling. Willie was quiet and skipped rocks across the water's surface. Tom thought of his father and felt the bulge of the Barlow knife in his pocket. The only prized material thing that Tom's father owned was a one bladed Barlow knife and he lovingly gave it to his son as he departed for the war. He knew that he might never see his son again. Grasping the knife in his hand, he pulled it out and started to carve on the smooth whitish-grey bark of a large beech tree.

The only two things that Tom could write slowly took shape in the bark. The year, 1862, and his name, were carved into the tree. But Tom didn't quite get it right, so Jarrell became "Jarars".

That night and that event faded into oblivion, but the tree lived long after Tom and Willie had gone on to their rewards. The land was eventually stripped and laid barren after the war, and other families eked out a living from the land during the 1880s to the 1930s. An economic depression in 1930 drove many from the land and soon the wasteland was purchased by the government for a bold experiment – a wildlife preserve on eroded land where little would grow, that would heal and become Piedmont National Wildlife Refuge.

One day 154 years later, in 2016, a lone deer hunter was easing along the creek bank when he thought he saw a face move around the other side of a tree. It looked so real, but it was only a shadow. But upon a second look, he did notice an irregular mark on the beech tree. Edging closer he was able to make out the date 1862 and the word "Jarars." Stunned by his discovery, he pondered what he had found and wondered who had done the carving. The beech gave him only a few precious clues, and much was left to his imagination.

The above scenario is only a guess as to the events leading up to the carving "Jarars 1862," found in a beech tree in Jones County on the Piedmont National Wildlife Refuge. The carving appears genuine and the history of the local area, along with dated grave sites, seem to substantiate the authenticity of the carving. Approximately two miles from the carving there is an old home site of the Jarrell family, which dates from the early 1800s and is today operated as a Georgia Historic Site.

Although the 1862 date is the oldest I have found, undoubtedly many more exist, waiting to be found by passers-by. I have found many dates from 1915 to the mid-1930s and some other unusual carvings. On one beech in Oaky Woods WMA is carved the word "bear" and below it is a carved bear paw, and the date 1933. There is also a figure of a man holding a moonshine bottle in one hand and a cigar in the other. I found the remnants of a moonshine still close by, along with water pool large enough for a good skinny dip, so I surmise that this was a gathering place for fun and relaxation.

The American beech tree (Fagus Grandifolia) lends itself well to tree carver of long ago as well as to more modern Kilroys. Its smooth grayish-white bark can be easily carved with a sharp knife, and the names, initials or dates are preserved in the bark as long as the tree lives. Dates back to the early 1700s have been reported on the trees along the eastern seaboard where early colonists settled.

Beech tree carvings were a primitive form of graffiti often created by Georgia pioneers. There has always been a strong desire for man to leave his mark on his surroundings. Early Indians often drew pictures of significant objects in their lives on the walls of their cave dwellings. The Egyptians drew both pictures and symbols on the walls of their tombs, living quarters and public buildings. Although modern man now uses printed materials and a host of other electronic devices to communicate, beech tree carvings recall a much simpler era when maybe a pen and a piece of paper wasn't handy. Perhaps early carvers were striving for just a little bit of immortality on the side of a beech tree.

But next time you are easing down a creek bank and notice a beech tree, look closely, because there may be a message there for you to ponder and appreciate from long ago!

CHAPTER 27
RARE PLANTS AND CHALK PRAIRIES OF OAKY WOODS

Georgia Aster, a protected plant, is common in Oaky Woods.

The Oaky Woods Wildlife Management Area, located in south Houston County on the west side of the Ocmulgee River, comprises about 13,240+ acres of pristine woodlands and prairies. The diverse physiographic areas within Oaky Woods contain not only remnant blackland prairies but upland forests, creek bottomland, and bog/swamp areas near the Ocmulgee River, according to Ed McDowell, who served on the Save Oaky Woods Advisory Board. McDowell says that within these areas many diverse plant populations thrive, especially in or near the six major prairies, along with eight rare species, one candidate for federal listing, and one federally endangered species.

Significant Plants:

1) The federally endangered Fringed Campion (Silene polypetala) is present as a small population on one site and one adjacent site. This represents the southernmost site for this plant in the Ocmulgee watershed and is of genetic significance as these populations differ from those in the Flint River and Apalachicola River ravines.

2) The bottomland along Big Grocery Creek contain disjunct Appalachian flora such as American Ginseng (Panax quinquefolius) and Trillium decumbens and evidence of American Chestnut (Castanea dentata) old trunks.

Oaky Woods WMA has a vast variety of wild flowers, including these prairie cone flowers that grow in the rare black prairie areas.

3) Several rare plants, including 6 state records, have been discovered in the blackland prairie habitat. Three-flowered Hawthorn (Crataegus triflora), thrives in sensitive transition zones between prairie grasslands and forested areas. Other rarities include the Dakota Vervain (Glandularia bipinnatifida), Umbrella Sedge (Cyperus acuminatus), Heartleaf Noseburn (Tragia cordata), Limestone Bedstraw (Galium virgatum), Drummond's Skullcap (Scutellaria drummondii), Orange Shrub Lichen (Teloschistes exilis), Georgia Aster (Symphyotrichum georgianum), and a state record, tiny mustard of blackland prairies known as Wedgeleaf Whitlow-grass (Draba cuneifolia).

4) Several hardwood forests contain outstanding examples of herbaceous "high pH" (calcareous soils) plants, such as the Green Violet (Hybanthus concolor), Yellow Climbing Milkvine (Matelea flavidula), Chapman's Wild Parsnip (Thaspium chapmanii), Underwood's Trillium (Trillium underwoodii), Shooting Star (Dodecatheon meadia), Early Meadowrue (Thalictrum dioicum), Woodland Phlox (Phlox divaricata), Cut-leaf Toothwort (Dentaria laciniata), and Lanceleaf Trillium (trillium lancifolium).

5) The hardwood forests contain an unusually rich mix of the Oak (Quercus) genus to include the following species: Black (velutina), Blackjack (marilandica), Cherrybark (pagoda), Chinquapin (muehlenbergii), Durand (sinuata), Laurel (laurafolia), Northern Red (rubra), Post (stellata), Southern Red (falcata), Water (nigra), White (alba), and Willow (phellos). Bottomlands along Big Grocery Creek upstream from Perimeter Road bridge contain state champion size Durand Oaks (Quercus sinuata). The presence of Durand Oaks makes Oaky Woods unique in Georgia. This presence defines a significant

coastal plain hardwood forest ecosystem not recognized until recently for the Atlantic Coastal Plain. Soils, geology, and the large remaining intact block of hardwoods, serving as a seed source, contribute to the ecological importance of these forests.

An article, "Research Shows Unusualness of Oaky Woods Chalk Prairies and Forests" appeared in the Macon Telegraph on October 12, 2009, written by S. Heather Duncan, and it pointed out the many special plants of Oaky Woods.

Duncan reported that "Lynch and another graduate student, Lee Echols (1), have been studying plants in Oaky Woods' forest and its prairies, respectively. What these unusual plant communities have in common is chalk. That's the common term for the limestone deposits left when Houston County was the shore of an ancient sea. Small white slabs of limestone still protrude from the ground in the woods and some have small bites of sea shells.

The prairies, which are frequently covered with waving asters, goldenrod and other wildflowers, were once commonly referred to as "black belt" prairies after similar formations in the Gulf coastal plain. But Echols' research, soon to be published (1), found enough distinctive geology and plants for the Oaky Woods formation to get its own, new category: Georgia Eocene chalk prairies. The Georgia prairies harbor a broad range of rare species, including some Echols documented for the first time in the state, and others that had never before been found on the coastal plain. The 43 acre site complex yielded 351 species in 219 genera and 89 families. Four species new to Georgia were documented. According to several state and federal rankings, twenty-three rare plant species occur within the study area; these include one federally endangered species (*Silene catesbaei*) and one candidate for federal listing (*Symphyotrichum georgianum*

Tom Patrick Ga DNR Botanist, shows off a rare trillium plant on a hike led by John Trussell

Echols also found Oaky Woods' first plant on the endangered species list, fringed campion, as well as two other flowers that are considered threatened within Georgia. "I found a ton of rare species there," he said, adding that the diversity of species was unusual for a study area of less than 100 acres.

Duncan added that, "In this forest and others in Oaky Woods, some "state champion" trees have been found. These are the largest known trees of their species in Georgia. Patrick and local Oaky Woods activist John Trussell believe there are more. Trussell, the founder of Save Oaky Woods, said he'll incorporate the new research into the tours he conducts for teachers, scout groups and others at the wildlife management area"

Footnote (1): S. Lee Echols and Wendy Zomlefer "VASCULAR FLORA OF THE REMNANT BLACKLAND PRAIRIES AND ASSOCIATED VEGETATION OF GEORGIA", Appalachian State University, 2002, masters thesis

Beautiful Trout Lillies broom in profusion in the springtime in Oaky Woods

CHAPTER 28
A HIKE IN OAKY WOODS

I've always had a sense of wander lust when it came to enjoying the outdoors. As a young man I loved to walk in the woods and ride my bike down dirt roads, often just to see what was over the next hill. Once on a deer hunt in Montana, I left camp and just decided to explore the beautiful countryside through the mountains. When I got back to camp that evening the GPS indicated I had walked 22 miles! My hunting buddies didn't believe me until I showed them a picture of an atv trail that was 11 miles away. I love the many simple things in life- the ability to walk in the woods and see the beautiful sights and sounds of nature. Cycling is just fast walking, when it's done on quiet roads. My enjoyment of cycling resulted in the book, "Road Biking Georgia" for Falcon Press in 2008, which profiles the top 40 cycling routes in Georgia.

My enjoyment of hunting and walking in the woods led me to explore Oaky Woods and over the many years I developed a strong personal connection to its many wild places, rare plants and beautiful hills and valleys. It was that personal connection that led me to start the group, "Save Oaky Woods" and consequently write this book. I am hopeful, that if you are reading this book, that you too can connect to Oaky Woods in a personal way that will inspire and renew your spirit!

From 2007 until today I have led many hikes into Oaky Woods so that others can explore and appreciate our wild places. I try to do a winter hike each year when the insects and snakes are less active and there aren't many hunters in the woods.

Left, rock piles, from pioneer days remain in Oaky Woods.

Visitors can now walk the roads, trails and fire breaks to get exercise in Oaky Woods. Cycling on bikes is allowed anytime the area is open, which is most of the year. If Oaky Woods is closed, the public can still walk in through the gates, but make sure you don't block the road with your vehicle. Anytime you're in the woods during hunting season, an orange vest is a good idea. Also make sure you take a cell phone, some emergency supplies like water and let someone know where you are going. Yes, you can easily get lost in Oaky Woods!

Currently, most people who use the site are hunters, but anyone can hike on the property. Visitors used to be able to come in for free, but due to regulation changes in 2017, visitors now must have a DNR Lands Pass, which is 30.00. A better option is to purchase a hunting or fishing license, which would be cheaper (15) or a one-day license (5) and these licenses help the Georgia DNR qualify for federal funds to operate.

The hikes we do highlight the area's unique history, particularly the fact that millions of years ago it was the bottom of an ocean.

A black Rat Snake checks out a birds nest in Oaky Woods, where its eat or be eaten!

Stephan Hammock, former Archaeologist at Robins Air Force Base, holds a couple of ancient sand dollars, about 33 million years old.

Back on a hike on February 22, 2014, we were joined by Macon Telegraph Writer Wayne Crenshaw and he wrote a story about his experience, "Hike Highlights Oaky Woods Unique History". Crenshaw wrote, "All throughout the woods where the hikers went were rocks embedded with sea shells. Hikers also saw a hill that had once been a coral reef, as well as the remnants of a moonshine still.

About 40 people went on the hike, including 15 students from Kings Chapel Elementary School in Perry. The students are part of a school club called Friends for Change, which emphasizes caring for the environment, said Ginny Caban, a music teacher who started the club.

"It was fantastic, getting the kids in nature," she said after the hike. "Some, like me, are city kids and have never experienced nature first hand like this. I think some of them will remember this the rest of their lives."

Laycee Wharam, a third-grader, said she learned a lot.

"The most interesting thing is knowing this was covered in water a long, long time ago," she said in Crenshaw's story.

The Lions Head on the Oaky Woods tour, which is an outgrowth scar, caused by a fugus on the tree

I also showed the hikers remnants of farming activity in the area before it turned into a forest, including rock piles and berms made by farmers.

The moonshine still on the hike was likely operated in the early 1900s. The large boiler is still there, with its sides expanded out from when federal agents blew it up. We visited areas that were once ancient coral reefs and steep hills were the kids could look for sand dollars and sea shells. We also visited a giant red oak that I call the Oaky Woods Sequoia. On this hike, like all the others, we had a great time in the outdoors, learned some news things about nature, got some great exercise and made some wonderful memories and many new friends!

A person who has been incredibly important in our Oaky Woods preservation effort is Alex Morrow, a Warner Robins attorney. Alex has helped me with many of our hikes and served as Treasurer and has been a very valuable ally for many years. I asked Alex why Oaky Wood was important to him and this is what he had to say.

"It could be pointed out that humans cannot exist on this planet without adequate vegetative cover to convert carbon dioxide into oxygen so well have a breathable atmosphere. Any green space we can keep in Houston County enhances the air quality and keeps us healthier. Scattered trees in the back yards of subdivision lots can never come close to equaling the oxygen production of a swath of mature forest such as Oaky Woods. Oaky Woods also eliminates tons of pollution from the air while it produces oxygen for us. Oaky Woods is busy cleaning our air and pumping fresh oxygen into our skies. We need to keep that pump running."

I asked Alex if there are other reasons to preserve Oaky Woods. "Yes", he said, "there are a vast number of citizens in Houston County who use Oaky Woods as a place of spiritual refuge. As the renowned naturalist John Muir put it, "Everybody needs beauty as well as bread, places to play in and pray in, where Nature may heal and cheer and give strength to body and soul alike." Oaky Woods is such a place. Human worries and the human clock are not important to the animals and plants of Oaky Woods. The plants and animals there have their own agenda and the sun, and the moon are their clocks.

Above- Alex Morrow with a variety of Oaky Woods wild flowers

When a human takes refuge in Oaky Woods, he or she enters a world where human, day-to-day concerns are not paramount. Oaky Woods is a place where, just for a little while, a person can forget his cares and find real peace, solitude, and quiet".

Alex made another observation, "Oaky Woods is unique in that it offers up sights and experiences not to be had elsewhere. Where else can the citizens of Houston County go to see a limestone bluff containing sand dollars that are from 30 to 38 million years old? In Oaky Woods, the citizens of Houston County can stand where whales once swam. The experience gives rise to a profound recognition of the age of the earth and the reality that monumental environmental changes have and can occur on our planet"

On Location at Sand dollar cliffs in Oaky Woods, creeping liverwort in background

I was blessed to have the help of my high school intern, Hunter Quintel, a very talented young man, during one of our hikes. I asked Hunter what made Oaky Woods special to him? He said, "I believe that Oaky Woods is special because these woods are of scientific and historical significance. These woods represent the culmination of changing water levels in the southeast and a resulting inland ocean, the eroding mountains of Appalachia which have provided for our current topography, the surprising diversity of the temperate forest ecosystem, the existence of a pre-colonized society, more recent proof of prohibition in our society, and current debate of development versus conservation of local wilderness".

Doves nest in Oaky Woods trees ten months out of the year. This mourning dove shelters her fledlings

He continued as he applied what he had learned in school, "Oaky Woods is a part of the Coastal Plain of Georgia and is shaped today by events of the past. Between 542 and 490 million years ago during the Cambrian Period, shallow seas covered the eastern edge of North America, and sediments, sandstones and shales were deposited due to erosion. Thicker deposits of limestone formed in these warm shallow seas in the Mississippian Period, and westward flowing rivers deposited sediment to the region as mountains eroded in the Pennsylvanian Period.

However, the tangible proof of Oaky Woods history comes from the Cretaceous and Pleistocene Periods primarily. Mollusk shells found in the woods today are remains of marine sediments from the Atlantic Ocean that covered Georgia as far north as Macon. Abundant echinoids fossils (sand dollars) and an early whale's fossils can be found today in the Eocene Ocala Limestone cliffs of Oaky Woods, which also come from this period, from about 32 million years ago. In the Pleistocene Period, large mammals including mastodons and mammoths inhabited Georgia."

Lightning is one of the most destructive forces in nature. Lighting hit this pine tree in Oaky Woods and peeled the bark down to the ground.

As we hiked through Oaky Woods, Hunter made some very insightful observations to me as we hiked for 2-3 hours as we walked among sand dollar cliffs, tall ridges and an old moonshine still. He observed. *"And just like that, around forty hikers became connected to Oaky Woods. Oaky Woods became tangible, memorable, and real to locals. This impact is the very nature of community involvement. Public interest in Oaky Woods is a major factor in the preservation and continuity of these woods. This determines the availability and accessibility of support through individual contributions and expressed representation in the state and federal legislature. Oaky Woods is the sum of the flora and fauna that make it up and the humans that care for and defend it."*

I could tell that Hunter will go far in the world.

Black Prairie areas are bleak in winter but will soon bloom into flowers in spring

I had the pleasure of sharing a short Oaky Woods hike with the popular Macon Telegraph writer Ed Grisamore and he penned a story, "Carvings are a Real Day at the Beech" on May 14, 2012, that got a very positive response. We walked down to what I called the "centennial Tree" because it had the carving of 9/3/1912 with the initials JW.

Unfortunately, the tree had been blown over and died. Another tree, below, was standing in 2012, but it too is now gone. It had a man holding a moonshine jug in one hand and a cigar in the other with the date 1933 below it. There was also a bear claw and the word, "Bear" carved into the bark, so they, too, thought bears were special. During the tough days of the depression, I can image workers retreating to the coolness of the stream late in the day to bathe in the creek and seek a little refreshment!

Grisamore appreciated the moment and said, "It is human nature to want others to know we were there. So, we mark our trails, stake our spots, sign the registry and dedicate a memorial to that moment in time. Kilroy Was Here. We leave handprints in wet concrete and draw hearts on sidewalks as a profession of love." Look for Grisamore's story on our webpage.

I have been a beech tree reader my whole life and always looked for the meaning of life in the life around me. The natural world is pretty amazing!

It is sad that the beech trees mentioned here are no longer with us, but all things must pass. We must learn, love and appreciate the life around us during our short journey through time.

CHAPTER 29

BE AWARE OF BEAR DANGERS

Most bears are as dangerous as your front porch sitting, biscuit eating Labrador retriever, and there has never been a dangerous bear encounter in middle Georgia, but you can never assume anything with wild animals. I have heard of a couple of instances where hunters were sitting in tree stands and had bears come up to the stand and either stiff around the stand or actually start to climb the stand, but they were trying to figure out the human scent and meant no harm to the hunter. Once the hunter shouted at the bear, it was off and running away.

On another occasion, years ago in Georgia, a deer hunter was reported missing. The next day he was found dead at the base of his tree stand and he had been mauled by a bear. But an autopsy determined the hunter was already dead went the bear encounter happened. There have been several instances where bears have been involved in deadly attacks in the USA in the past.

In September 2014, in West Milford, New Jersey, a hiker who was killed by a bear, took pictures of the animal just before the attack. The pictures show the 300-pound black bear approaching the group of hikers in West Milford's Apshawa Preserve on Sept. 21, according to authorities.

The photographs are from the phone of Darsh Patel, the 22-year-old Rutgers University student who was killed by the same bear just a short while later, said Lt. Keith Ricciardi, of the West Milford Police. The phone was later recovered with a puncture mark from the animal's teeth, according to investigatory records.

Chief Timothy Storbeck said in previous interviews that Patel and four of his friends had begun walking into the preserve that afternoon when they were met by a man and a woman coming the other way. The pair warned the larger group about a bear following them. The couple walked away, leaving the group of five to talk about what they were going to do. They eventually walked farther into the woods. The five stopped when they saw the bear, that was 300 feet away

This poor photo of a large black bear is the last picture on Darsh Patel's cell phone. Unfortunately, he took it just seconds before the bear attacked and killed him.

The five pictures taken from Patel's phone show the bear from approximately 100 feet, looking toward the hikers but still behind a fallen log, authorities said.

The hikers turned around when the bear kept approaching, authorities said. But the bear caught up with them, eventually closing to within 15 feet, investigators said. When the bear reached that proximity, the group split up running in different directions, they later told police investigators.

Patel at one point lost his shoe and was last seen climbing a rock formation as he hollered for his friends to continue, with the bear right behind him. The group of four fled the woods and called 911, according to police records.

Emergency responders came upon Patel's body about four hours later. The bear was in the area, authorities said. Eventually, a police officer shot and killed the bear. An autopsy showed that Patel was mauled by the bear. Human remains were found in the bear's stomach and esophagus, and human blood and tissue were found underneath its claws, authorities said.

The death of Patel was the first confirmed instance of a person being killed by a bear in New Jersey. Some 60 such fatal attacks have occurred in North America over the last century, experts said. However, the attacks on Patel can still be considered "one in a million," they added.

Black bears were virtually eradicated from New Jersey by the 1960s but have since rebounded to a population of about 2,500.

In the situation in New Jersey, the group made a mistake by splitting up and running. Had they stuck together, shouted at the bear and chased it off with rock and big sticks, they probably could have forced the bear to flee. Bears become dangerous when they are fed by people and see people as sources of food. When you do see a bear, you should not run. A lot of times that's a first instinct, but it can trigger a chase response,

Experts say that the best response is to just back off slowly and they'll usually just run away. If you come around a corner and surprise them, just get up on a rock or log and make yourself look bigger, throw something at them, blow a whistle, wave your arms; just appear bigger than they are. Don't try to follow them with a camera or let your dog off leash. This writer has had numerous encounters with black bears over the years, some at close range, and the bears have always run away very quickly.

Several years ago, in Oaky Woods, I was bow hunting and stalking along a trail when I heard a lot of limbs breaking nearly above my head. A large bear was in the top of a pine tree, eating muscadines from a vine that had grown high in the tree. The bear saw and smelled me and decided to exit the tree in a hurry. It slid down the tree, breaking limbs and creating a shower of pine bark in the air. It hit the ground with a loud thud, only 15 feet from me, then ran into the woods. I was armed with my bow, but the bear was only trying to get away and meant me no harm.

Another time I was bow hunting in Oaky Woods, when I had a bear sow and cub approach my ground blind. They got within 15 feet and suddenly the sow smelled me and led out a loud huff, then the sow ran off one way and the cub the opposite direction. Wondering what would happen next, I waited, and about 30 minutes later the sow returned to the spot, with its nose to the ground. It was tracking its cub, like a hound dog, and soon followed the trail of the cub over the hill. Sows have strong maternal instincts and will care for their cubs for 2-3 years after birth.

A good thing to remember to avoid problems with bears is to not leave any food sitting around if you're camping. Secure it, tie it up on a tree limb, or put it in a car trunk, because bears have an excellent sense of smell. Even something like shampoo or toothpaste can attract them. Securing food sources and properly disposing of trash usually prevents any problems.

Bears are big animals and require a lot of food on a daily basis, so they are on the prowl for food since their natural food sources, such as berries, and acorns are seasonal. Bears also dig up yellow jacket nests to eat the larva. In the fall, they will graze on green wheat fields, peanuts or even peanut hay bales. But never trust a bear to turn down a free meal it smells at a campsite.

When you enter a wildlife area, you're entering prime habitat of bears and lots of other animals, so the potential is always there to see them, because we're visiting their realm. People need to be aware and need to use extra precaution and common sense around bears.

Bear safety tips

Remember these tips when visiting forests and other woodlands in north Georgia, around the Okeefenokee Swamp or in central Georgia, around Oaky Woods or Ocmulgee WMAS, where bears are present

- Do not store food in tents or items with an odor (such as shampoo and toothpaste), and do not eat in tents.

- Keep a clean campsite by properly disposing of food scraps and garbage.

- Do not leave food or garbage inside fire rings, grills or around your site.

- Never leave food or coolers unattended, even in developed picnic areas.

- If bear-proof containers are not available, store food and garbage inside, high in a tree that is away from camp, or in a car trunk.

- Avoid camping and hiking alone in the backcountry.

- Make noise to avoid surprising a bear.

- Never approach a bear or other wild animal.

- Do not hike in the dark.

- Consider Carrying EPA-registered bear pepper spray when in an area were bear /human encounters are likely, but that is not likely to occur in middle Georgia. I never saw the need to have bear spray in central Georgia, but I am unusually armed, mostly concerned about rabid animals, which I have encountered several times. Always carry a cell phone for emergency communications, but in an emergency situation, don't expect a call to 911 to save you. Use your brain and be prepared.

- If a bear approaches, move away slowly; do not run. Try to get into a vehicle or a secure building, but in an outdoor setting, you'll probably be away from any shelter.

- If you are attacked by a black bear, try to fight back using any object available and shout at the bear. Playing dead is not appropriate, as the bear means to kill and eat you. For more info go to https://www.nps.gov/subjects/bears/safety.htm#Spray

Violent bear encounters in Western NC and East Tennessee- few examples

June 2015: A teenage boy is dragged from his hammock and mauled by a bear while sleeping in Great Smoky Mountains National Park.

August 2011: A Candler man and his dog were injured in a scuffle with a bear, which started when the bear attacked the dog.

May 2010: A bear was euthanized after biting a tourist in Great Smoky Mountains National Park.

December 2009: A captive bear in Cherokee mauled a bear handler.

October 2009: A llama at an eastern Buncombe farm was attacked by a bear and had to be euthanized.

June 2009: A Black Mountain woman was hurt while trying to protect her dog from a bear.

August 2008: A bear was shot and killed after attacking an 8-year-old boy in Great Smoky Mountains National Park.

April 2006: A bear attacked and killed a 6-year-old girl in Cherokee National Forest in East Tennessee.

In the western states, like Montana and Wyoming, bear attacks occur every year, but as I mentioned before, there has never been a bear attack in Georgia.

WHAT TO DO IF YOU FIND A BEAR IN YOUR BACK YARD? You wake up and find your dog has treed a bear in your back yard, what do you do? The best thing to do is to bring the dog inside and leave the bear alone. It will soon exit the tree and return to the woods on its own. It doesn't need any help from the Georgia DNR or area law enforcement. The problem arises when we call the neighbors and say "Hey, I've got a bear in my yard" and for hours we admire the bear in the tree and soon a crowd is drawn in to the event. If you report the bear, it suddenly become a problem "nuisance bear' that someone in state or local government has to deal with, which could have unfortunate consequences for the bear.

If you really want to help the bear, just leave it alone and it will return to the woods! You should consider why the bear was in your yard, and usually it's because you have a food source such as cat or dog food, food in your trash, a bird feeder or wildlife feeder. Remove the food source and the bear will be gone too. Several years ago, a home owner in Bonaire found a bear in a tree in his back yard, attracted by his dog's food. He called Georgia DNR and they came out, shot the bear with a tranquilizer gun and obviously, a 20- foot fall from a tree is not good for the bear. It was removed to Twiggs County. That was range of about 20 miles and across the Ocmulgee River! A few days later, the same bear was back in the same yard and in the same tree! Bears have great memory recall of territory over large distances.

So, traveling 20 miles and swimming the Ocmulgee River was no barrier to getting that good dog food! Once again, the bear was removed from the tree and this time it was taken a much further distance away. The solution to the bear problem is to remove the food and the bear will be gone!

CHAPTER 30
KNOWLES LANDING A GREAT ASSET TO MIDDLE GEORGIA

If you want to reach the section of Oaky Woods that is 10 miles up the Ocmulgee River, you must put in a boat at Knowles Landing and travel upriver. Like-wise, if you want to access Oaky Woods downstream, you must put in at Knowles landing and travel downstream several miles, but the main section of Oaky Woods is usually best accessed through the land roads and you don't want to wander on private lands. When you're not hunting, this section of the river provides good fishing for bass, crappie, and bream. You will also find that mullet run up the river and can be caught in the upper Ocmulgee. Always remember that there is little boat traffic on the river and if you break down, it could be a long wait for help, so be prepared! Make sure to have an extra shear pin for your prop, a cell phone, extra gas, and food and water. Try to bring a fishing partner along, so you have some help if trouble arises.

Many years ago John Knowles, left, and the author teamed up to renovate the Ocmulgee River Boat ramp park at highway 96 in Houston County

You might be wondering; how did Knowles Landing get its name? It has been many years since John Knowles and I teamed up to improve the Houston County boat ramp, located where Highway 96 crosses the Ocmulgee River.

Looking back, I want to revive old memories by running most of a column that I wrote for the Warner Robins Daily Sun Newspaper in 1995 and give readers some updates.

Daily Sun, October 1995: "It's been a long time coming, but the newly renovated Houston County boat ramp on the Ocmulgee River at Highway 96 is now officially the "Knowles Landing". Recently the Houston County Commissioners voted to name the boat ramp after John E. Knowles, a long time Bonaire resident and devoted Ocmulgee River fisherman. The Commissioners took their action after a delegation of Bonaire residents, led by Dave Davidson, Seventeen Burdine and Ray Wheelus recommended that the boat ramp area be named for Knowles.

At 10:00 on October First, a gathering of local officials, Knowles' family and friends met at the boat ramp area to officially dedicate the location to Knowles. Comments were made by County Commission Chairman Sherrill Stafford, Dave Davidson and John Knowles.

Knowles said "I am deeply honored by the County's decision to dedicate a project, like the newest boat ramp on the Ocmulgee River, after me. So many people contributed to its financing, planning and labor who easily deserved the honors. But seeing the excitement and enthusiasm of this announcement on the faces and in the voices of all my friends and neighbors is the most moving of all. I just did not think so many people would have been so approving and I'm so grateful to the Commissioners and all my friends and neighbors in Houston County."

Jokingly, Knowles said "I hope people don't get the idea that the fishing must be extra good right now. Maybe we could put up a sign out here that says, 'Fish here!'" But seriously the crowd knew that Knowles wants to share the gift of the river and its beautiful natural environment with all the citizens of Houston County.

After the dedication comments, the group was treated to the traditional fisherman's lunch of sardines on saltine crackers! Just kidding, although that would have suited Knowles just fine. His wife, Nadine T. Knowles, provided the group with a very nice decorated cake that had "Knowles Landing" printed on the top, along with doughnuts and cakes.

Those in attendance included Commission Chairman Stafford, Commissioner Larry Snellgrove, Sheriff Cullen Talton, Conservation Officer Tony Fox, DNR Regional Fishers Supervisor Les Ager and State Senator Sonny Perdue and this writer. Other friends in attendance were Ronnie Beard, Ray and Myra Wheelus, Seventeen Burdine, Sam Favst, Jimmy and Tina Evans, Tom Williams, Neil Oeanman, Don Hill, Ford Wilson, Lizzy Ward, Barbara Mynott and Charline Smith. Several of Knowles three children and 10 grandchildren were also present.

The present boat ramp area is almost a dream come true for Knowles and the many other fishermen who have fished the Ocmulgee River for many years. The old, original boat ramp was inadequate from the day it was built many years along the D.O.T. Right of Way, under the 96 bridge. The ramp was shallow, making boat launching difficult and it frequently filled in with sand. But Fishermen are known for getting by with next to nothing and were glad to at least have access to the river. Knowles, Wheelus, Chuck Lawson and Charles Sloan were among the earliest fishermen to say the boat ramp needed replacement, but their recommendation went unanswered until former County Commission Chairman (now Commissioner) Jay Walker took an interest in developing the area. The short road leading to the old boat ramp was on DOT right of way, but very neglected. This sort of made it a "no man's land" with Law Enforcement and a difficult proposition, thus many people were reluctant to visit the river.

This writer has been a frequent visitor to the Highway 96 boat ramp for many years and was disappointed in its lack of usefulness. The access road along Highway 96 was always in very poor condition and the boat ramp was awful! The situation really got bad when law enforcement had to look for lost fishermen or other emergencies and had difficulties launching a boat. It represented a common problem that every sportsman complained about, but no one did anything about it!

But John Knowles provided this writer additional inspiration to tackle the problem. Back in 1993 I was writing a story about Ocmulgee River catfishing for Georgia Sportsman Magazine and contacted John Knowles, a good river fisherman, to go fishing with me and catch some catfish. Knowles was happy to help me, and we wrote up a good article about the experience in the magazine. But during our fishing trip he commented to me, "This boat ramp sure needs a lot of work, don't you know some people that can fix it up?"

Knowing that the replacement of the boat ramp was long overdue, I began a plan to remedy the problem. The first thing I did was contact Jay Walker, then the Houston County Commission Chairman, and ask for his help. Jay and I visited the boat ramp on a sunny day and he agreed it needed a lot of help. He said, "Why don't you work on a plan and bring it before the Commissioners?" Thus, I sat out to address the problem in the following months. After reviewing county land maps, I concluded that we should buy 3.2 acres of land surrounding the old boat ramp and Ocmulgee River and got Brent Cunningham, a well-respected land surveyor, to draw up a map of the proposed purchase.

I consulted with Mike Long, the Houston County Legal Attorney, and he started purchase negotiations, keeping the Commissioners informed on the progress. Initially, the owners did not want to sell, but Mike Long convinced them that public access to the river was a very legitimate public safety issue and finally the owners consented to the sale. I consulted with Tommy Stalnaker, the Director of Public Works, and he was ready, willing and able to get the boat ramp and parking lot work done. Les Ager, the Regional DNR Fisheries Supervisor, offered his office's assistance in getting in the concrete pillars for the boat ramp.

After all the preliminary work was done, I attended a County Commission Meeting in Perry and presented the plan to them, which they approved. Thanks to Commissioners Jay Walker, Sherrell Stafford, Larry Snellgrove, Charlie Steward, Houston Porter and Archie Thompson for addressing the need for a new boat ramp.

The property was leased to the DNR and soon Les Ager's crews came in and constructed the new boat ramp. Although recurring high waters, including the flood of '94 have hampered further development, in recent months the public boat ramp area has undergone significant improvement due to the leadership of Chairman Stafford and hard work of public works Director Tommy Stalnaker and his crew.

The parking lot area was recently paved, and 34 parking spaces have been marked off. In addition, large granite rocks have been placed around the perimeter to prevent erosion and drainage pipes have been installed. While the parking area was being constructed, Knowles, Wheelus, Burdine, Davidson and friends fixed a fish fry for the workers in appreciation of their work. The Bonaire Community has really gotten behind the boat ramp to be lengthened and picnic tables to be installed.

Ray Wheelus, who was very active in promoting the need to rebuild the boat ramp, says "It's now a real nice boat landing and it's something we have needed for a long time. John Knowles is a good local river fisherman and we're all proud to have it named for him."

Seventeen Burdine, another boat ramp supporter, says "Now that the area is fixed up we know that local people will take more pride in the area and we hope more people will come out and enjoy the river. It's a nice place to fish or just watch the river flow by. We were glad to recommend the area be named for Knowles because he loves to see people have a good time fishing, especially kids."

"Knowles is a World War Two Vet and retired from Robins Air Force Base and is part of America's Finest Generation. He was delighted and humbled by the boat ramp being named for him and says he accepted the honor in behalf of all the many people who made the new landing a reality.

Recently, as I spoke to Knowles near the beautiful Knowles Landing sign near the river bank he said, "You know, 50 years from now people will come to this river and wonder who that Knowles fellow was. They might think he was a Senator or something to have this nice boat ramp named after him, but he wasn't so. He was just a fisherman who loved this river and just wanted to share his joy with others."
This is the end of the old newspaper column, so now here are some present time comments.

Sometime in the future, the boat ramp will be moved to the north side of the Ocmulgee bridge when the road is expanded, and I hope it will be improved again. But the name Knowles Landing will always remain. It is a fitting tribute that this place be named for John E. Knowles, the good river fisherman, who as a young man, answered the call to duty to defend own country from German aggression. As an 18-year-old soldier he carried a 30 caliber BAR auto rifle across North Africa and Italy and participated in many battles along the way. He received a Purple Heart for some injuries, but too many of his good friends died and their memories are forever etched in his soul. Luckily many of his Telfair buddies survived the war, but of the 38 soldiers who were drafted with him from Telfair County in 1942, he is the only one still alive, as of 2018. That brings him sadness, but he's very proud of his "Band of Brothers" who fought for freedom and the greatest country in the world, he says. So next time you're fishing on the Ocmulgee River, remember that freedom is not free, and everyone must do their part to keep America strong. Knowles and his friends have helped to build a living legacy for all present and future Ocmulgee River fishermen.

CHAPTER 31
GEORGIA'S YAZOO LAND FRAUD AND THE BUILDING OF AMERICA

When Houston County, Georgia, was founded in 1821, it stretched all the way to the Flint River, and later several other counties were broken off from it. Although Houston County was larger back then, it was puny compared to the original size of the state of Georgia. King George of England, in 1733, gave the Georgia trustees all the land from the Atlantic Ocean to the South Seas, which meant the Pacific Ocean! But why leave a cozy life in England and travel to a far -away uncivilized land?

Larry Morgan, left, Mayor of Louisville, with the Author, in front of city mural painting. Louisville, Georgia, was named for King Louis 16th for his help during the American Revolution

They came for land and opportunity! The life was hard on the frontier, but they were a hearty bunch. Our first immigrants into the Eastern USA and Georgia came primarily from England, Ireland, Scotland and Europe. If your family has been in the USA many years, you probably descended from these first settlers. When Edward Oglethorpe planned the Georgia Colony he had first planned to help people in debtor's prison, but by the time he got the land charter from King Edward 2nd, he decided to plan for good success and dropped the debtor's prison idea.

He instead handpicked the 116 men and women of good character, but poor and looking for new opportunity, who would travel to Georgia on the ship, "The Ann". These folks were gunsmiths, bakers, farmers, carpenters, and tailors with valuable skills. When they landed in the area that would become Savannah in 1733, the settlers had to forage the woods for edible game animals and streams for fish or go hungry. They only brought limited supplies from England. Just about everything they needed they had to kill, catch or make from locally available raw materials. With an axe to fell trees, they built the first log cabin homes in Georgia.

Thankfully, Oglethorpe landed in an area with friendly Native Americans and the local chief, Tomochichi helped the settlers to survive. As more people arrived, they took over available land suitable for farming and signed treaties with the Indians, who were very sparsely populated in the area and our westward expansion took off! Interestingly, Oglethorpe had some utopian ideas, and banned liquor, slaves, lawyers and Catholics from the new Georgia colony, but those restrictions did not hold up for long!

Although Georgia had a unique land problem in that the state was blessed with territory that stretched all the way to the Pacific Ocean, the boundary was shortened to the Mississippi River in the Treaty of Paris in 1764 which ended the French and Indian war. This was not much of an issue as the land was wilderness and only inhabited by Native Americans, but after the Revolutionary war was won in 1783, Georgia's politicians began to think of that land as a low hanging fruit, ready to be picked for profit, while some others wanted the land given to the federal government

Although Georgia owned huge amounts of land, there was no way for the new, and low populated colony to develop or control lands that were hundreds of miles away. Georgia politicians tried to form counties in the new territory and later attempted to give the lands to congress, but both efforts failed. Georgia also arranged a deal in 1779 to sale 25 million acres to three private companies, but when Georgia demanded the funds in gold or silver, rather than paper money, the deal collapsed.

In 1794, support for a deal increased in the restless Georgia legislature, as the young state needed the funds to operate its government. Georgia Governor George Mathews, on January 7, 1795 signed the Yazoo Act, named for the river in Mississippi which flowed through the lands. Georgia sold 35 million acres to four private companies for $500,000. These lands would eventually become the states of Alabama and Mississippi. It sold for about 1.5 cents per acre! By comparison the Louisiana Purchase sold for 3 cents per acre and Alaska sold for 2 cents for acre! The leader of the Yazooists, Georgia's Federalist U.S. senator James Gunn, had arranged the distribution of money and Yazoo land to legislators, state officials, newspaper editors, and other influential Georgians to grease the deal with money to insure its passage. Soon the public got wind of the wheeling and dealing and the mood turned sour!

News of the Yazoo Act and the illegal wheeling, dealing behind it aroused anger throughout the state and resulted in a large turnover of legislators in the 1796 election. The new legislature promptly rescinded the act and in a public display of regret, burned the original bill papers on the courthouse grounds. Joel Chandler Harris, an editor for the Atlanta Constitution, and famous for the Uncle Remus stories, put a strange twist on the burning papers episode.

He wrote, "When the officers of the state meet to destroy the records on the courthouse lawn, an old man, a stranger to all present, rode up on a horse. Lifting up his voice, as feeble as it was, he said he had come to see an act of justice performed and said that the fire to destroy the records should come from heaven. He drew from his bosom a sun magnifying glass and put the suns' rays upon the papers, igniting them. He then got on his horse rode away never to be seen again." It's unknown how the politicians really burned the burned the papers, but Chandler told a good story!

The state tried to return the money for the land, but by this time, however, much of the land had been resold to third parties, who refused the state's money and maintained their claim to the territory. Many of the owners were wealthy and well -connected northerners. The dispute between Georgia and the land companies continued into the 1800s. The state of Georgia ceded its claim to the region to the U.S. government in 1802. Finally, the issue was reviewed by the U.S. Supreme Court, and in 1810 Chief Justice John Marshall ruled in Fletcher vs Peck that the rescinding law was an unconstitutional infringement on a legal contract (Footnote 2). Congress awarded the State of Georgia 1,250,000 in 1802 and the claimants received 4,000,000 in 1810. By 1814 the government had taken over the land which became the new states of Alabama and Mississippi.

The Yazoo Lands Rescinding Act of 1796 had another repercussion as the U.S. government promised to help remove the remaining Creek Indians from Georgia. The western expansion of settlers across Georgia was meet with some resistance from Indian groups and caused deaths on both sides of the struggle. In the treaty of Indian Springs in 1821, Chief McIntosh, a mixed breed of Irish/Indian blood, signed a treaty giving white settlers access to thousands of acres of land in middle and western Georgia. This land would become Houston County and many others. The Indians had many chiefs, and some were opposed to the treaty deal and they promised to kill any chief that gave up any more land. After McIntosh signed the treaty, a group of about 150 creeks raided his farm on the Chattahoochee River in April 1825 and killed him.

Although he was considered a sinner by the Creeks, the white settlers considered him a saint and today the McIntosh Reserve Park is open to the public in Carroll County, near Whitesburg. A monument there states: "To the Memory and Honor of General William McIntosh-The Distinguished and Patriotic Son of Georgia whose devotion was heroic, whose friendship unselfish and whose service was valiant. Who negotiated the treaty with the Creek Indians which gave the state all lands lying west of the Flint River. Who sacrificed his life for his patriotism" Erected by William McIntosh CHAPTER D. A. R. Jackson, Georgia, 1921." The first state Park in Georgia, Indian Springs Park, near Jackson, is where the 1821 treaty was signed.

In Georgia's Yazoo fraud era and early settlement days, there were plenty of both saints and sinners. In exploring my roots through the Sons of the American Revolution, I discovered two relatives involved in the Yazoo land deal. One was a cousin, Lemel Lanier, who rightly voted against the original Yazoo Act and my direct SAR ancestor grandfather, Lewis Lanier, was elected to the Georgia Legislature in 1798 after the controversy. I never would have discovered these ancestors had I not been involved in SAR! My goal is to get you to explore your own family roots through the Sons of the American Revolution (SAR) or Daughters of the American Revolution (DAR). You never know what you'll find as your family roots have many stories to tell! For more info, go to sar.org or dar.org and let your own journey begin! Although a very important story in the history of Georgia and the Southeast, the Yazoo land controversy has faded into history. (This article, by the author, first appeared in "Sons of the American Revolution' Magazine, spring 2017).

Footnote one: Georgia Encyclopedia," Yazoo Land Fraud" George Lanplugh , 2002

Footnote two: 'The Great Yazoo Lands Sale: The case of Flecher v Peck," Charles Hobson

CHAPTER 32
EXOTIC/ INVASIVE PLANTS OF OAKY WOODS

I grew up in central Georgia and thought that kudzu, mimosa, china berry, azalea and camellia were just part of our great southern culture! But I quickly learned that some of the plants that we see growing in Oaky Woods and Georgia are not native to our area and are, in fact, quite exotic! Many plants were brought here in the late 1700's and early 1800's from all over the world and they found our climate very agreeable and grew like weeds! Often it is hard to credit, or blame, any one person for the exotic species of plants that now grow across the south. We can suppose that early world travelers would see a plant that they thought was "cute or unique", then take a rooting and stuff it in their bag for the trip home to the USA. I think we have all been guilty of seeing plants in today's modern garden center and imagining how that pretty plant would look in our home landscape!

In the early American colonies, there was little thought given to spreading undesirable plants and diseases and it was easy to bring plants into the country. There was little to no bag inspections for contraband, that are so common today. Plants arrived into America ports and their spread would begin. As early settlers moved into Georgia from the earlier settled colonies to our north, like Virginia and South Carolina, grandma would take her shovel and dig up some of her favorite plants to bring with her!

Many years ago, I found some colorful and unique glad flower bulbs growing at a site in Oaky Woods that was probably the old horse stage coach stop at a place called Buzzards Roost. More recently, I found the same colored bulbs growing at a site in Monroe County, 30 miles to our north, that was an old stage coach stop. It is highly likely that these flowers might have found a small empty space in the stage coach luggage bin when the driver went home to see his wife! Lovely flowers to express love never go out of style!

Ride down some of the dirt roads in Oaky Woods and you will see crepe myrtles growing along the roadside. These were popular among early settlers and were readily available from seeds. The common crepe myrtle (*L. indica*) from China and Korea was introduced *circa* 1790 to Charleston, South Carolina, in the United States by the French botanist André Michaux. He planted them at Middleton Plantation and other sites along the Carolina coast. He has also been credited with bringing in the first camellias and sasanquas into the USA. From these fairly simple plants, we now have thousands of different varies and color combinations that have been developed by research gardeners and plant hybridizers.

These heirloom glad flowers can be found at the old stage coach stops in Houston and Monroe Counties

Mimosa, or Persian Silk tree, are now common across the south. It's ferny leaves and fluffy pink flowerheads cover the tree in summer make it a garden-worthy plant, as do the light sweet fragrance emitted by the flowers, which attract bees. Seed pods that resemble flat beans follow the flowers and persist into winter. The tree can easily become invasive, so cut back root sprouts and clean up the seed heads. The seeds are eaten by birds and often survive the trip through their digestive system, thus they have been widely spread and become established trees throughout our woodlands.

Another exotic tree that seems to have nine lives is the chinaberry tree. As you can imagine, it's native to southern China, and is related to the mahogany tree. Cut it down and it will re-spout from the roots and the seeds remain viable for several years. Chinaberry is often seen growing in "chinaberry groves" were numerous trees have taken over the landscape in small sections and shaded out other vegetation.

Chinaberry is also mildly poisonous, so be careful about picking the flowers or having it around children. In the old days, kids would often use green or dried chinaberry seed as sling shot ammo and I can tell you they work well! The fruit is marble-sized, light yellow at maturity, hanging on the tree all winter, and gradually becoming wrinkled and almost white. The seeds are also spread by wildlife and are probably food for squirrels, chipmunks and other critters. Like many exotic species, it has a "Jekyll and Hyde "personality. Some good, but mostly bad, so don't plant it!

Another plant that is common in Oaky Woods is Japanese honeysuckle vine. It was brought into Ohio from China, Japan and Korea in the mid 1800's and quickly spread across the south. It has yellow and white flowers and is easy to spot as it creeps across the ground and climbs into brushes and trees. Although an evasive plant, it is very useful as a wildlife plant for deer and other animals as it stays green all year when little other food is available in the woods. There are many other invasive plants, too numerous to cover them all, but I have to say a few words about kudzu, probably the most well known of our invasive weeds.

My grandmother, Leila McDuffie Smith, had stories about a lot of things that she shared with us kids, so here is her Kudzu story. We often slept in rooms with no air conditioning when we visited with the windows open, but we did have screens to keep out the mosquitoes. She warned us not to sleep too close to the window or the kudzu, which was very fast growing, would sneak into the room, get around our necks and strangle us! Needless to say, we slept across the room from the window!

Kudzu was introduced at the 1876 World's Fair Centennial Exhibition in Philadelphia, as a novelty plant to feed cattle or grow over the porch and provide shade. It was really good at providing shade as it grew over barns, telephone poles and trees. But farmers found little use for a vine that could take years to establish, was nearly impossible to harvest and couldn't tolerate sustained grazing by horses or cattle. But in 1935, as dust storms damaged the prairies, Congress declared war on soil erosion and enlisted kudzu as a primary weapon. More than 70 million kudzu seedlings were grown in nurseries by the newly created Soil Conservation Service. To overcome the lingering suspicions of farmers, the service offered as much as $8 per acre to anyone willing to plant the vine. Railroad companies planted it to stop erosion along rail road tracks, so it got a lot of help to spread and it's never going away! It has a reputation as the plant that ate the south, but it's not done yet! Kudzu is common in Oaky Woods and the deer and wild pigs will eat the tender young shoots if they get hungry enough!

Who knew the kudzu had pretty flowers?

CHAPTER 33

FLYING SQIRRELS, SPANISH MOSS, CYCADIAS, MISELTOE, HONEY SUCKLE, DOGWOODS AND SANDHILL CRANES

There are a few things in the southern woodlands that are pretty special and deserve close examination. So, let's take a look at some of my favourite outdoor delights, then you can appreciate them too! I first became aware of flying squirrels when I was a very young man and was camping out with friends, Al Childers and Ted Blackmon in my tree house. We were about 10 years old and were passing time, cooking up some grub and telling ghost stories. It was about 10 pm and we only had a single candle for light, so it was already kind of spooky! After a scary story, we were all settling down to sleep in our camping bags, when we heard a loud "Thump" on the side of the tree house. Naturally that got our attention and then we heard this loud scratching noise as, if something was trying to get inside the tree house! Good golly Miss Molly! It was time to abandon ship!

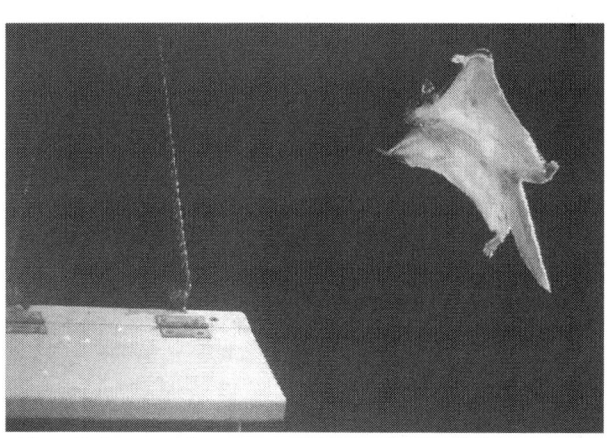

A flying squirrel comes sailing into a bird feeder to grab a snack

We piled out of the tree house and found a strong flashlight to inspect the outside of the structure. We saw a critter running up the side of the tree house and just take a flying leap into the night air! We were young, but not stupid, and figured out the flying critter was not a ghost but was a flying squirrel! They are fairly common in Georgia, but are rarely seen by the casual observer, since they usually come out late in the evening. I usually see them nesting in my blue bird boxes and they will also nest around chimneys and any hole they can find into home attics. When you see one, you'll be very impressed with the flying squirrel's ability to jump out of a tall tree and glide in the air for long distances.

The southern flying squirrel (GLAUCOMYS VOLANS) is the smallest of all tree squirrels with a normal body weight of two to four ounces and body length of eight to 10 inches. This squirrel is easily distinguishable by the loose fold of skin called a patagium between the wrist of the fore and hind legs. The southern flying squirrel does not actually fly as its name implies but rather uses this flap as a combination parachute and sail or glider wing. Flying squirrels sports a very silky coat that is grayish brown above with a white under-belly. Large black eyes and a long and densely furred tail are characteristics of the southern flying squirrel. Capable of gliding distances of 80 yards or greater, southern flying squirrels can turn or change the angle of descent. Just before landing, the squirrel drops its tail and lifts its forequarters, slackening the flight skin to serve as an air brake. Although southern flying squirrels are agile and sure-footed in flight, they are relatively clumsy on the ground. Their call is faint and bird-like and can be heard in early evenings in the spring and summer seasons of the year.

They can be found throughout the eastern United States except for northern New England and the southern tip of Florida as well as west of Minnesota, eastern Kansas and eastern Texas. Southern flying squirrel numbers are stable or increasing across the southeast. Although rarely observed, they are common in most forested areas. Southern flying squirrels prefer mature hardwood forests but are found in most forested habitats. Woodpecker holes are favoured nesting sites for the southern flying squirrel, but they may build a summer nest of leaves, twigs, and bark. Active all year, FLYING SQUIRRELS may remain in its nest in extremely cold weather. In the winter, groups of up to six individuals may den together in one tree hole. Their home range may span four to 19 acres.

Southern flying squirrels are thought to be the most carnivorous of the squirrels; however, animal matter consumption is miniscule at times. Their diet includes some birds and nestlings as well as eggs, carrion, and invertebrates. The typical diet for the southern flying squirrel includes nuts, buds, fruits, berries, mushrooms, and seeds. Southern flying squirrels mate from December to March and

June to July. They are capable of reproduction at the age of six to eight months but do not mate until 10 to11 months of age. The gestation period is 40 days. Many times, I have found them nesting in my blue bird boxes!

SPANISH MOSS-It drapes from trees and just seems to say to the casual observer," You're in the South Now"! It is a bromeliad, which means it is in the same taxonomic family as, wait for it, pineapples and succulent house plants!

Various Native American tribes, including the creek Indians in Georgia and the Seminole, have used Spanish moss for a variety of purposes. When the outer coating of the plant is cleaned away, tough, black, curly inner fibers are exposed. These strong fibers were useful in many ways. The fibers were woven into a course cloth that was used for bedding, floor mats and horse blankets. The fibers could be twisted into cordage that was used as rope. The ropes were used to lash together the poles that composed the framework of housing. The dried fibers were used to remove scum in cooking. The process used to strip off the outer coating is still used today. It consists of placing bundles of the green moss into a shallow pond for six weeks, long enough for the outer coat to rot away.

Spanish Moss hangs of tree branches all over the south and we southerners love it!

Dry Spanish moss was used for fire arrows. The moss was wrapped around the base of the shaft, lit on fire and then shot from the bow. The moss was also an ingredient in the clay that was used to plaster the insides of houses. Fresh Spanish moss was gathered, soaked in water and stuffed into dugout canoes to keep them from drying out and splitting. The Natchez tribe of Louisiana played a game that used fist-size balls that were stuffed with Spanish moss.

The plant was boiled to make a tea for chills and fever. There is evidence that Spanish moss was used over 3,000 years ago to make fire-tempered pottery among southern Indian tribes. Although the moss burned away during the firing, the distinctive pattern of the fibers is still evident in the clay pottery. Spanish moss is a native, perennial epiphytic herb. It is not Spanish, nor a moss, but a flowering plant. The slender, wiry, long, branching stems (reaching 8m or more) grow as suspended, bluish-gray streamers and garlands draping among tree branches and sometimes telephone lines and fences. The plant and is not parasitic, as is often thought, but attaches itself to trees for support. The plant has no roots but derives its nutrients from rainfall, detritus and airborne dust. Like anything in the outdoors, it can be home of ticks and redbugs/chiggers, but because it's usually high in a tree the infection rate is low.

CICADAS- Recently, I got out of my truck down in Oaky Woods and heard a low roar that sounded like heavy machinery running. I moved around a bit, then realized the loud noise was cicadas singing! The trees were full of these amazing insects! Cicadas begin life as a rice-shaped egg, which the female deposits in a groove she makes in a tree limb, using her ovipositor. The groove provides shelter and exposes the tree fluids, which the young cicadas feed on. These grooves can kill small branches.

A cicada slowly removes itself from its hard shell. Soon it will spread its wings to fly to find a mate.

Once the egg hatches the cicada begins to feed on the tree fluids. At this point it looks like a termite or small white ant. Once the young cicada is ready, it crawls from the groove and falls to the ground where it will dig until it finds roots to feed on. Once roots are found the cicada will stay underground from 2 to 17 years depending on the species. Cicadas are active underground, tunneling and feeding.

After the long 2 to 17 years, cicadas emerge from the ground as nymphs. Nymphs climb the nearest available tree and begin to shed their nymph exoskeleton. Free of their old skin, their wings will inflate with fluid and their adult skin will harden. Once their new wings and body are ready, they can begin their brief adult life.

Adult cicadas, also called imagoes, spend their time in trees looking for a mate. Males sing, females respond, mating begins, and the cycle of life begins again. For more info, go to cicadamania.com. There are 190 species of cicadas in the USA, with different life cycles so every year you'll see them flying around and trying to hum up a mate. The circle of life continues and that's a very good thing!

MISTLETOE- Why did my mom sent me to the woods to get some mistletoe for Christmas decorations when I was just a little boy? I doubt she understood the reasons, other that it was pretty. But from the earliest times mistletoe has been one of the most magical, mysterious, and sacred plants of European folklore. It was considered to bestow life and fertility; a protection against poison; and an aphrodisiac. (The berries are poisonous- so don't eat them and keep away for children!) Mistletoe is especially interesting botanically because it is a partial parasite (a "hemiparasite"). As a parasitic plant, it grows on the branches or trunk of a tree and actually sends out roots that penetrate into the tree and take up nutrients. The mistletoe of the sacred oak was especially sacred to the ancient Celtic Druids.

Mistletoe was long regarded as both a sexual symbol and the "soul" of the oak. It was gathered at both mid-summer and winter solstices, and the custom of using mistletoe to decorate houses at Christmas is a survival of the Druid and other pre-Christian traditions. In the Middle Ages and later, branches of mistletoe were hung from ceilings to ward off evil spirits. In Europe they were placed over house and stable doors to prevent the entrance of witches. The traditions which began with the European mistletoe were transferred to the similar American plant with the process of immigration and settlement.

In the south, we really like the custom is kissing under the mistletoe! Kissing under the mistletoe is first found associated with the Greek festival of Saturnalia and later with primitive marriage rites. They probably originated from two beliefs. One belief was that it has power to bestow fertility. In Scandinavia, mistletoe was considered a plant of peace, under which enemies could declare a truce or warring spouses kiss and make-up. Later, the eighteenth-century English are credited with inventing the kissing ball. In the south, we like mistletoe because we love traditions!

HONEYSUCKLE AND NATIVE AZELEA- In the springtime, the scent of honeysuckle and native azaleas drift through the branches in Oaky Woods and it can be intoxicating. Trumpet honeysuckle (L. sempervirens) and Japanese honeysuckle (L. japonica) are two of the most ornamental of the honeysuckle vines. They can be red, pink, white or red and are an important wildlife food, especially for deer in the wintertime.

A giant Swallowtail Butterfly, top left, feeds on a native azalea, R. Canescens, in Oaky Woods

Native azalea is pink to almost white and is a deciduous shrub, losing its leaves in the winter. It likes to grow in moist bottom lands and is one of the prettiest flowers in the woods. The light pink variety of native azalea is the Piedmont, or R.Canescens and has a very sweet smell. You may also run across the Florida(R.Austrinum) or Flame Azelea(R. Calenduleum), or several others.

Dogwoods are among the prettiest springtime flowers in Oaky Woods

DOGWOODS- When the dogwoods bloom in the spring, it just makes you want to sing. Spring has sprung, and life is beginning a new! The bright white flowers really cheer up the woodlands and if you're a fisherman, it signals that the crappie are spawning and biting!

SANDHILL CRANES- Often mistaken for geese, sandhill cranes migrate through Oaky Woods and all of middle Georgia in the early spring and fall. Our local geese population does not migrate, and they were transported here by truck by the Georgia DNR in the 1970's from northern states where they had become a nuisance. They fly low from pond to pond or to grass fields and can be very domesticated in urban areas.

Sand Hill Cranes migrate through middle Georgia by the thousands every spring and fall with a high-pitched call.

Sandhill cranes are very wild and breed in Canada and northern areas, then migrate to the gulf coast for the winter. They can fill the sky by the thousands and make a distinctive high -pitched call. I love to see them come through middle Georgia and find it reassuring that the cycle of life continues in the wild! Once endangered, they are now plentiful. Presently there is no hunting season for sandhills in Georgia, but they are hunted in a few western states.

I do hope you and your family will get outdoors soon and enjoy Oaky Woods!

A rare January snow covers this sign in Houston County, Georgia

For a long walk in Oaky Woods, try one of the many permanent fire breaks that run through the property.

"A simple walk in the woods is a wonderous exercise. How lucky we are to walk upon the earth for our brief existence, breath the fresh air, feel the dirt beneath our feet and see the blue sky above. Troubles melt away and life is Good"
– John Trussell

ABOUT THE AUTHOR

John T Trussell, B.S. Criminal Justice, Georgia Southern University; M.Ed., University of Ga, is an award winning Outdoor Writer, having published both in print and online more than 1,000 articles over the last 30 plus years. He has received many awards from the Georgia Outdoor Writers Association and Southeastern Outdoor Press for writing and photography. He is past President of the Georgia Outdoor Writers Association. He writes regularly for Georgia Outdoor News, Georgia Game and Fish and several other magazines. He has been actively involved in many conservation projects and was the founder of Save Oaky Woods, was a member of the land search committee for Flat Creek Public Fishing Area, served on The Go Fish Education Center Advisory Board and led the effort to rebuild the Houston County Boat Ramp park, now known as Knowles Landing. He has also had an active career in Law Enforcement while fishing and hunting across the USA whenever possible. Some of the stories here were gathered from the public relations effort to "Save Oaky Woods", which he led as a non- paid volunteer. For his conservation work and writing, he was inducted into the Georgia Outdoor Writers "Hunting and Fishing Hall of Fame" in 2015, which is housed in the Charlie Elliot Wildlife Center. He is also a UGA certified Naturalist.

Made in the USA
Lexington, KY
12 November 2019